The Hidden and True
Pneumatology

The Hidden And True Pneumatology
Translation and Introduction Copyright © 2023 Steve Savedow
ISBN 978-1-915933-12-6 (Hardcover)
ISBN 978-1-915933-13-3 (Softcover)
ISBN 978-1-915933-14-0 (Digital)

Hardcover edition printed by TJ Books, Cornwall.

A catalogue for this title is available from the British Library.

Steve Savedow has asserted his moral right to be identified as the author of the introduction to this work.

All rights reserved. No portion of this book may be reproduced by any means without the permission in writing of the publisher, except in cases of short passages for purposes of review and citation.

Published by Hadean Press
59a Cavendish Street
Keighley, West Yorkshire
BD21 3RB
www.hadeanpress.com

PNEUMATOLOGIA OCCULTA ET VERA

The Hidden and True Pneumatology

An Obscure 17th Century Grimoire Text for Conjuring Spirits to Reveal Hidden Treasure, Derived from a Manuscript of the Mystical Spanish City of Salamanca

Translated from the German into English, edited, with footnotes and introduction by

Steve Savedow

This book is dedicated to the memory of Samuel and Belle Ginsburg, also Christopher Frost, Sam, Mae, Randy and Barry Savedow; with special thanks to Jacqueline, Michael, and Linda Faye Savedow, Scott and Benjamin Savedow, Muffet Robinson, Patti and Samantha Frost, and Chris Buchanon.

Special thanks also to Erzebet Barthold, Dis Albion, and David Rankine for their invaluable assistance, and to Alexander Cummins for writing such a generous foreword.

Contents

Exhuming Treasure: A Foreword by Dr Alexander Cummins   ix
New Introduction by Steve Savedow   xix
Morals: historical introduction to this writing   xxix

THE HIDDEN AND TRUE PNEUMATOLOGY

   Preface   2

   Prayer   11

   Preparations for a perfect authority of spirits   18

      Light to find buried treasure   23

      Magic Glass Mirror   24

      Virgulta Divina   25

   The days of the month in the year preferred for the citation of the spirits   29

   The true and right way in which spirits are challenged and spoken to   31

   The angels and devils   38

   The good angels, who rule every day of the week   48

   Final Incantation   71

   Appendix A: Names of the Angels and Spirits Listed in this Book   77

   Appendix B: A Selection of Treasure Spells In Various Grimoire Texts   93

   Appendix C: Biblical References   106

   Bibliography   108

Exhuming Treasure
A Foreword by Dr Alexander Cummins

The grimoire before you – *Pneumatologia Occulta et Vera* – deals in conjuration of the (relatively) pious treasure hunting variety. It identifies itself as a product of the 'Mystical Spanish City' of Salamanca – that bastion of rumoured black magic and blacker books of sorcery – and brings together instructions on preparations necessary to summon spirits, as well as the practical working of 'lights' to find buried treasure and the constructions, consecrations, and uses of both a 'magic glass' (earth-)mirror and a divining rod employed in the detection of literal buried treasures.

Casting fresh light upon this little manual of spirit-trafficking – drawn from the pages of the older sister-tome of *Das Kloster* known as the *Zauber-Bibliothek* (*The Magic Library*) – translator and commentator Steve Savedow offers us an Englished form of this text along with carefully-placed commentary and several helpfully compiled appendices of treasure-hunting operations and pertinent supplemental material. Steve's introductory commentary touches on the Cyprianic lore of Salamanca and other sites rumoured to house a secret Black School of necromancers-in-training. He offers us valuable comparisons across the wider grimoiric corpus of the forms of pious conjuration found in this *Hidden & True Pneumatology*, as well as considering more necromantic tomes. We are also more fully contextually situated by a brief survey of Iberian treasure-hunting, elemental earth spirits, and the construction and operation of earth-mirrors.

The grimoiric text of the *Pneumatology* offers us – *inter alia* – a survey of operative pre-modern European demonology, practical advice on best circling practices for calling and directing devils, angels, and planetary spirits, as well as some fascinating insights into the rather combative model of conjuring and exorcising treasure spirits themselves. It features both typical tenets, techniques, and tools of such sorcerous treasure-seeking operations, as well as some more unusual – not to mention fascinatingly folk magical – methods, *materia*, protocols, and advice.

Hidden & True Manners of Conjuring Spirits

The cast of spirits named and worked through this *Pneumatology* are at once familiar and somewhat idiosyncratically constellated. Those conversant with traditional European demonological spirit lists and catalogues will note the appearance of the recognisably important 'hellish spirits and princes, Acheront, Astharoth, Magoth, Asmodi, Beelzebub, Belial, Aimaymon, Paymon, Egym, with your subordinate custodians and servants'.

The text's demonological *dramatis personae* evidences influence from a range of grimoiric sources including the *Book of Abramelin*, especially drawing from its extensive hierarchies of subordinates and superiors. It also carries a profound influence of the *Heptameron* (if not its earlier medieval sources) in emphasising the operational importance of planetary timings and astrological entities.

In spite of the fact that – or perhaps precisely because – the endeavour of finding, disenchanting, and recovering lost or secreted treasures of the earth might seem a rather materialistic venture, the circle-work of the *Pneumatologia* seems especially pious; especially in comparison to, say, the grubby treasury of fell Faustian experiments for mobilising devilish forces for the same ends. *H&TP* insists in fact that the operator not scribe or rely on any demonic names or seals for their circle.

Our present grimoire actually provides a few important *notae* on the protocols for drawing and working a circle, not only for the central operator or magister, but also for the roles, functions, and assistances that their 'fellows' can offer and fulfill. One rather trinitarian-flavoured tip worthy of particular note involves bringing along three assisting 'fellows' who all share the same name. While the importance of things done in threes is found throughout European cunning-crafts of charming and conjuring, this particular sympathic naming convention for conjuring by circle seems most unusual and perhaps even unique to the strains of folk magic that influenced our present *Pneumatology*.

The *Pneumatologia*'s conjurations, citations, and dismissals (not to mention its *notae* and advice) elucidate some expectations of chaotic spiritual resistance when conjuring for treasure. *H&TP* cautions indeed that the proper methodology does not (at least immediately) engender harmony between the operator and the spirits, but rather will cause visions of ravens to fly at the conjuror who must hold fast against such wicked tricks of these possessive and withholding treasure guardians who are noted to reproach those who seek their troves.

The previously-noted piety of *Pneumatologia*'s protective circles are more understandable given this expectation of an antagonistic response; and once more the importance of being sanctified above and beyond reproach. It should also be noted that this grimoire makes particular endeavour to detail the specifics of what the nine-day period of clean living to be observed prior to an experiment of conjuration actually looks like: covering the particularities of oft-repeated but also oft-ill-defined concepts like 'chastity', 'mercy', 'charity', and sober and moderate speech and conduct.

Pneumatological *Materia*

The *Pneumatology* also especially shines in its down-to-earth techniques and practical treatments of various recommended *materia magica*, which once more demonstrate an admixture of influences from both more formal ritual grimoiric sorcery and folk magical observations and implementations. Most of these injunctions and instructions are eminently practical. The operator is encouraged, for instance, to draw the sanctifying Holy Name as well as mark the four additional pentacles about the circle 'in the four corners' in chalk, and is therefore reminded to *actually carry chalk* on their person.

The recommendation of the use of earthen pots or vessels for incensing is once more reminiscent of the working manner of at least the *Heptameron* if not both its predecessor and descendant text families of conjuration chapbooks and manuals. The suffumigation method advanced by *H&TP* recommends two incenses – one to lure spirits and one to dismiss them – which clearly draws on Paracelsian considerations of sympathical and antipathetical *materia*, savours, and actions in spirit-work.

The wand-lore promulgated by our present *Pneumatology* draws on established northern European cunning, recommending a hazel wand of a single finger's thickness measuring a single cubit in length, which should be recognisable to those versed in the English cunning-crafts recorded and circulated via Reginald Scot's *Discoverie of Witchcraft* and similar sources. It should also remind of us of comparable operations empowered by petition to the Three Magi to fabricate and conjure hazel rods of detection, as well as popular English treasure dowsing with 'Mosiacal' batons of hazelwood. The wands of the *Pneumatologia* even bear some comparison with (and certainly contrast to) early modern French conceptions of similar sorcerous detectorism with 'Jacob's rod'. The *Pneumatologia* also demonstrates an influence of a particularly French medievalism in its appellation of such divining rods as the 'Staff of Caroli' or '*Stab Caroli*' i.e. the rod of Charlemagne.

One particularly noteworthy component prescribed by this *Hidden and True Pneumatology* concerns the garments to be worn when performing its sorcerous works. Unlike most grimoires of pious spirit conjuration, which recommend one sports the white clerical robes either directly acquired or taken from, or worn by a priest, or at least one exactly reminiscent of a priest's – and indeed unlike even the nigromantic Black Books' instructions to dress in dread Saturnal black – the *Pneumatologia* insists that one must wear a shirt which 'you must have inherited from your ancestors'. This particular instruction cannot be said to be a commonplace occurrence in European books of conjuration, although somehow it brings to mind the '*Stammgeist*' of the Faustian grimoiric mileu; a term which seems to have been variously translated 'haunting-spirit' and 'tribal-ghost'. Perhaps another flash of some *wyrd* old folk necromancies' ancestral veneration, propitiation, and empowerment in these grimoiric papertrails.

Familiar ritual conjuration protocols are also repeated however, insisting that this inherited shirt be properly 'clean and washed'; rehearsing more Paracelsian considerations that 'both the evil and the good spirits love cleanliness; the latter because they are without the pure spirits; the former, however, because they were also transfigured in uncleanness, and then also have bodies transfigured in their damnation, and the same can be driven out and irritated with nothing more than stinking and unclean things.' Once more, this grimoire evinces an evocative friction between clean and unclean, sanctified and sordid.

Another prime example of this motif should be noted. This handbook of treasure-hunting magics employs familiarly early modern grimoiric components of *animalia*: specifically the blood of a white dove and a mixture of bloods of a black lamb and a white dove. These materials seem exclusively considered practically for their value as a writing medium and tool or ingredient of conjuration. There are no instructions pertaining to offering the animal's body or life to any spirit, merely the insistence that one uses this kind of blood for your ink or ritual circle. The lack of protocols for how to dispatch them or even how to extract vital fluids – which can be found in many bloodier grimoiric texts – seem to confirm this is not animal sacrifice in the strictest sense, but rather an employment of a component of suitable sympathetic virtue.

The mixture of black lamb's and white dove's blood seems to hold a rather more ritual purpose than the ink, for it is to be sprinkled outside the circle. It is somewhat ambiguous whether this ritual action simply further consecrates and empowers the circle itself, or if it actually allures spirits, or even if it empowers the chalked characters about the circle mentioned immediately before the sprinkling instruction; or any/all of the above, or indeed none of these reasons! While the exact reasoning behind it might remain uncertain, such a blooding of the circle itself is not an unusual feature of even the more pious of early modern conjuration manuals, yet once more the *H&TP* characteristically foregrounds a combination of the chthonic and the celestial, in both the mixture of the bloods of white and black animals, and indeed the blending of the blood for sprinkling with holy water. We should note while perhaps easily considerable as an inherently violent and thus self-consciously "wicked" act to many modern sensibilities, such animal bloods – and we should note the lamb and the dove both are thoroughly Christological animals – were employed ritually for sanctifying to God as well as for sacrificing to demons.

This combination of the enlightening and the obscuring, the good and the bad, might even be likewise read out of the formulations for the 'light to find buried treasure'. The protocols for manufacturing and employing these magical candles evince an influence from a range of Albertine works concerning the *'cerra flav'* or "blonde wax", and instantiate a noteworthy mixture of the divine (frankincense) and the diabolic (sulfur) in their constitution; which, considered emblematically, seems a consistent characteristation of this grimoire's manners and methodologies in general.

The magical use of wax lights to locate buried treasure is also highly reminiscent of an operation involving a Lunary talisman detailed in Israel Hiebner's 1698 treatise of scientifical astrological magic, *Mysterium Sigillorum, Herbarum & Lapidum*. Hiebner's planetary sigil of the Moon consists of a cast metal medal stamped on one side with a classic 9x9 lunar *kamea* or number square and on the other – in a fascinatingly literal take on image magic – with a topologically-accurate rendering of the physical Moon's surface complete with the scars and craters of our satellite's beautifully weathered face. Along with being enclosed in a white silk bag and 'hang'd about the neck in the Influence of the Moon' which 'preserves from and cures all Lunar Sicknesses', such a sigil could also be employed in more specific magical experiments, including discovering hidden riches:

> 'If you put a Wax-Candle in the middle of this Sigil, and carry it round about the House and other Places, where the Candle suddenly goes out, there is hidden Treasure. If there be now a Lunar or Saturnal influence... [which Hiebner not only elects and lists earlier in his book but also at this juncture helpfully cites to cross-reference such timings]... then Dig with good courage, and you will find Treasure.' Israel Hiebner, *Mysterium Sigillorum, Herbarum & Lapidum* (London, 1698), 190.

This operation is pertinent to mention in comparison to the Albertine ceremantic operation of the *Pneumatologia* itself; which, as you can soon read, also locates treasure (and more specifically 'money') by where the light extinguishes. We may also contrast it to another experiment found *The Supreme Black, Red and Infernal Magic of the Egyptians and Chaldeans* – helpfully excerpted and appendixed by Savedow in this present edition of the *Hidden & True Pneumatology* – for discovering 'the object of your yearnings' by following the flicker of a properly-prepared human tallow candle.

Beyond close comparative study of the specific techniques of pyromantic and ceremantic divination, these various workings demonstrate a variety of candle-dowsings to be popular practices, and clearly adapted to range of necromantic and astrological modalities of operating. That Hiebner ascribes this operation a Lunary sigil also highlights a centrality of planetary virtues and spirits in pre-modern folk magics that the *Pneumatologia* also clearly shares.

Hidden No Longer

The present edition of the *Hidden & True Pneumatology* is helpfully laced with concise and clarifying footnoted commentary, presenting translator's notes and original phraseology for unusual and noteworthy terminology, as well as bibliographic citations and comparisons across the wider grimoiric corpus. Steve has also compiled a useful index of named spirits with some biographical concise information for quick-reference support.

This present edition of the *Pneumatologia* also boasts a modest trove of its own, in the form of a comparative appendix of treasure spells, compiled from the *Grimorium Verum*, the *Black Books of Elverum*, various *Keys of Solomon*, the *Black Dragon*, the Albertine *Egyptian Secrets* and *Petit Albert*, as well as an operation from a forthcoming translation by Savedow himself of the *Treasure of the Old Man of the Pyramids*.

These excellent supplemental resources are rounded out with a final appendix touching on the Christian theology and psalmic magic referenced in the text, offering further support for enterprising magicians to put these experiments into practice.

THE HIDDEN AND TRUE PNEUMATOLOGY

Upon leafing through the entire book you now hold in the hands of your attention, you can indeed quickly discern that both the presentation of the *Pneumatologia* translation itself and the valuable appendices, commentary, and indexes offer contextualising and operationalising assistance for the magical reader and worker alike to understand these workings and indeed to fold them into their own magical practice. This text and its careful footnoting, indexing, and appendixing all tend especially towards assisting the reader and worker in understanding at least some of the practicalities of *cunning* rather more than the ostentation of mysticism.

The *Hidden & True Pneumatology* can be characterised partly by its familiar grimoiric components, influences, and structures; and partly by its unexpectedly folkloric traces of techniques and tools, such as the three names and the hand-me-down ancestral shirt. Much more can and should be written and spoken about this work, but for now I will bid you on your way with some of the wisdom of *Pneumatology* itself: 'But with that, dear reader, here all long-windedness flees, and you may carry only the core of the incantations and what belongs to them.'

May you find treasure enough for all.

Dr Alexander Cummins
New England, 2023

New Introduction

BY STEVE SAVEDOW

THIS OBSCURE LITTLE grimoire text is nicely tucked away in a collection of rare German treasures, dating from the early nineteenth century and compiled by Georg Conrad Horst. The *Zauber-Bibliothek*, or *Magic Library*, is an interesting compilation of grimoire and theurgia texts, as well as witchcraft and paranormal titles. The *Zauber-Bibliothek* compiles subjects "... of Magic, Theurgy & Divination, Sorcerers, Witches & Witch Trials, Demons, Ghosts & Spirits",[1] and is collected somewhat in the tradition of the better-known *Das Kloster*, which is a popular accumulation of rare German magic texts, grimoires, mythology, erotica, Faustian mythos, and classical fairy tales, etc., in twelve "stout" volumes[2] produced a few decades later.

Pneumatologia Occulta et Vera was transcribed in the first volume by Horst from an unusual manuscript, said to be dated about 1660 (according to the editor), but other than this one source, apparently very little information as to its provenance exists. It is so obscure that I could not find any references to it, either on the internet or from the books in my own substantial grimoire library, which is one of the reasons that I became quite obsessed with it. I assume it was taken from a German manuscript, although it is mentioned that it was found in Spain, from the University of Salamanca. In fact, there are a few references to Salamanca—a city in western Spain, and the capital of the province of Salamanca in the

---

1 *Zauber-Bibliothek* in six volumes, published in Mainz, Verlag Florian Kupferberg, 1821–1826.

2 *Das Kloster. Weltlich und geistlich. Meist aus der ältern deutschen Volks-, Wunder-, Curiositäten-, und vorzugsweise komischen Literatur,* editor Johann Scheible, published in Stuttgart, 1845–1849.

community of Castile and León—in the editor's preface. The University of Salamanca is a Spanish higher education institution, founded in 1218 by King Alfonso IX. It is the oldest university in the Hispanophone world and one of the oldest in the world in continuous operation.

> In Salamanca was the famous Cueva de Salamanca, or Cueva de San Ciprián, a cave that served as the sacristy—below the Iglesia de San Ciprián (St. Cyprian's Church) in which was told that the devil taught black magic to the university students of Salamanca. Salamanca is one of the more important universities in Spain and one of the oldest ones. The cave was open until the "Catholic Queen" Isabel ordered to close it circa 1500. In 1580 the church was definitively destroyed, but part of the sacristy (that was at the same time the cave) survived and is still today there. Salamanca and Toledo were the most famous magical centres in the Iberian social imaginary and this probably had real foundations, and this tradition spread all over the world, including Europe. (In South America the word Salamanca means a cave in which is practiced magic.[3]

The title of the manuscript, *Pneumatologia Occulta*, was possibly a deception during a time when such materials were considered taboo, being at risk during (what is known as) "the burning times", when occult and ritual magic texts were subject to the flame, especially in European countries. The title reveals little as to the actual purpose of the text, which is the conjuration of spirits in order to locate and acquire hidden treasure, liberating said treasure from some magical being by disenchantment.

---

[3] Felix Francisco Castro, "The Books of Saint Cyprian" <https://danharms.wordpress.com/the-books-of-saint-cyprian/>.

THE HIDDEN AND TRUE PNEUMATOLOGY

The science of pneumatology refers to a particular aspect of Christian theology that focuses on the tradition of the Holy Spirit. The word itself comes from the Greek πνεῦμα (pneuma, meaning "spirit" or "breath"; metaphorically it is a description of a non-material being or influence), and λόγος (logos, or "teaching"). This involves the work and study of the Holy Spirit, including Christian teachings on new birth, sanctification, the inspiration of prophets, spiritual gifts or charismata, spirit-baptism, and the permanent presence of God or a spiritual force in the heart or soul, in regard to the Holy Trinity.

The text has a definite Christian influence, opening with a lengthy Catholic prayer in the tradition of the *Sworn Book* and *Grimoire of Pope Honorius*, and also the *Enchiridion of Pope Leo*. But prior to this prayer is an interesting pagan invocation of Hecate which is offered in Latin; it is fairly morbid, mentioning "...drive through corpses to the grave...". This text also draws from Hebrew, as well as Greek, mythology, and additionally other classic grimoire texts. There are also various other Latin phrases, including a quote attributed to Saint Cyprian, which was most likely taken from some version of the well-known *Book of Saint Cyprian, or Sorcerer's Treasure*.[4]

There is a tradition among grimoire texts of including spells or formulas involving the acquisition of "hidden treasure", sometimes referred to as simply gold and silver, although obviously there are different interpretations of the term "treasure".[5] The *Book of Saint Cyprian* includes very interesting material relating to hidden treasures, especially regarding the *Mouros/Mouras*, supernatural spirits that live in forests, and also near the waters of the rivers and on sandy beaches. While there is much to consider here, the translator José Leitão states: "The *Book of St Cyprian* appears

---

4 Hadean Press, 2014, translated with commentary by José Leitão.

5 In David Rankine's *Book Of Treasure Spirits* (Avalonia, 2009), Rankine states "Thus the magician requested treasure 'of Gold & Silver, Coin, Plate, Bullion, Jewels, or other Goods and Chattels'".

time and time again in the 'Moura' legends as the utmost, certain method of treasure disenchantment. The *Book* has managed to imbue itself beautifully into this mythical continuum, which can actually be traced to the most remote antiquity of Iberia."[6] Later he quotes from the book itself, "All treasures and enchantments of the ancient kingdom of Galicia deposited by the *Mouros* and the Romans in underground lairs."

In order to acquire hidden treasure that is concealed by magical means, such as by spirits known as *Mouras* or Gnomes, for example, there are several different spells or formulas in various classic grimoires, although this particular text is fairly unique. I am also including an appendix in this volume, detailing a selection of spells from various grimoire texts for locating and acquiring treasure.

In *The Key of Solomon the King*, it is noted, "The Earth being inhabited, as I have before said unto thee, by a great number of Celestial Beings and Spirits, who by their subtilty and prevision know the places wherein treasures are hidden, and seeing that it often happeneth that those men who undertake a search for these said treasures are molested and sometimes put to death by the aforesaid Spirits, which are called Gnomes."[7]

In the same vein, *Le Petit Albert* states, "Those who are occupied in the discovery of gold and silver mines observe some ceremonies to gain the benevolence of the gnomes, so they are not opposed to them in their undertakings. Experience has taught that they are very fond of perfumes, and this is why the wise cabalists ordered them to be specific to each day of the week in relation to the seven planets. As I know from experience, many people have succeeded in discovering treasures by means of these perfumes. I am willing

---

6 Loc. cit., page 271.

7 Translation by S.L. MacGregor Mathers, London, 1889; see also the superior new edition, *The Veritable Key of Solomon*, edited by Stephen Skinner and David Rankine, Golden Hoard Press, 2008/2017.

in favor of my readers to give them the real way of making them, so they can be agreeable to gnomes, guardians of these treasures."[8]

Finally, in the *Sworn Book of Honorius*, under the heading "concerning the spirits of the earth", it is stated, "You can work with the terrestrial spirits using the same method described in the preceding work, if the suffumigations and the names are altered, as well as the circle and the seals. (2) We will speak about these spirits briefly here. They are the most ugly and full of all kinds of wickedness. (3) Their nature is to root out the roots of trees and crops, to guard and preserve treasures hidden in the earth, to cause earthquakes, to destroy the foundations of cities or castles."[9]

In order to provide a bit of context, especially for those readers who are not familiar with grimoire texts, consider the following as a bit of Classic Grimoires 101. There are a variety of different types of grimoire texts which fall into particular categories. A "true grimoire" usually involves demon or spirit evocation, or "conjuring" of a spirit (or spirits), in order to acquire something or to gain knowledge on a specific subject, as in the infamous *Grand Grimoire* (or *Le Dragon Rouge*) and *Grimoirium Verum*.[10] There are grimoire texts which draw upon Jewish or Hebrew traditions, such as *The Book of Abramelin*, *The Sword of Moses*; the best known is probably the *Goetia* (part of the *Lemegeton*, or *Lesser Key of Solomon*). There are Christian grimoires, for example the *Enchiridion of Pope Leo III*, the *Sworn Book of Honorius*, and the *Great Grimoire of Pope Honorius*. Also, there are Arabic grimoires such as the *Picatrix* and Thabit ibn Qurra's *On Talismans*. There are folk magic grimoires such as the "Little Albert" (*Le Petit Albert*) and the *Sixth and Seventh Books of Moses*, and additionally there are even fictional or fabricated grimoire texts, such as the *Necronomicon* (of

---

8 Translation by Steve Savedow, see Appendix B.
9 Translation by Joseph Peterson, Ibis Press, 2016.
10 See the bibliography for details of the grimoire texts cited here.

the Lovecraftian Cthulhu Mythos)[11] and the *Ninth Gate* (from the movie of the same name starring Johnny Depp), based on the novel *The Club Dumas* by Arturo Pérez-Reverte). The *Pneumatologia Occulta et Vera* may be classified as a "true grimoire" of the Germanic Christian tradition, but it also includes influences from other sources (such as its Spanish origins in the city of Salamanca, as well as Hebrew and Greek mythology), as is not uncommon.

The first reference to specific entities in this text pertains to the seven "Olympian" or "Olympic" spirits, notably from the *Arbatel* (first published in Basel, Switzerland, 1575, first translated from the Latin by Robert Turner, 1655; more recently published by Ibis Press, 2009, translated, edited and annotated by Joseph Peterson), the full title being *The Arbatel: Concerning Magic, Or, The pneumatica* [spirit] *of the ancients along with the magi of God's people, as well as the magi of the Gentiles, for the illumination of the glory of God, and his love of mankind*. The third septenary of the *Arbatel* deals with the "Olympians", the spirits of Olympus or Olympic spirits, and these are "heavily influenced by the writings of Paracelsus".[12] There are also listings of spirits or "demons" in *Pneumatologia Occulta*, including the dukes and kings from *The Book of Abramelin*[13] as well as those of the *Goetia* or *Lesser Key of Solomon*,[14] and the *Heptameron*'s[15] talismans for the days of the week also match with those in *Pneumatologia Occulta*.

---

11 There is even a fictitious bibliographical history and chronology detailed in *Beyond the Wall of Sleep* by Howard Phillips Lovecraft, Arkham House, 1943.

12 Peterson, *Arbatel*, page xi.

13 Translated by S.L. MacGregor Mathers, London: John Watkins, 1889; see also the new translation, *The Book of Abramelin*, Ibis Press, 2006, revised & expanded 2nd edition 2015, compiled & edited by Georg Dehn, translated by Steven Guth.

14 Originally transcribed by S.L. MacGregor Mathers, and later published by Aleister Crowley and "the Society for the Propagation of Religious Truth", 1904; more recently translated by Joseph Peterson, Weiser/Red Wheel, 2001.

15 See *Heptameron: or, Magical Elements of Peter de Abano together with the Arbatel of Magic*, Ouroboros Press, 2003, translation by Robert Turner, 1655.

In the text itself there are various rather obscure aspects, such as "the light to find hidden treasure", which is a candle made with "cerra flav" (Latin for "blonde wax"), and utilizing frankincense and sulfur, that I also later discovered in the *Albertus Magnus*.[16] There are also specific instructions for the usage of various incenses for each planetary angel, as well as the recipe for incense to be brought into the protective circle during the final ritual to acquire hidden treasure. There is also another recipe for incense to drive the wicked spirits away, as well as the equivalent to "the license to depart", after the ritual has been completed.

There is also a talismanic circle, called "Erd-Spiegel" or "earth mirror". It is a hexagram in a circle, utilizing the sigils of the planets in the triangles of the hexagram, and the talismanic sigils of the angels of the days outside the hexagram, as well as the Hebrew letters *Yod Heh Vau Heh*, with the solar symbol for the Sun in the center.[17] Later in the text, there is a protective "magic circle" with hexagrams, talismanic sigils, and Hebrew names of God with Christian names (some in Latin) of Jesus, Jehova, etc., written around the outer circumference of the circle.

Also, the text includes instructions for creating a "divining rod" presented with numerous sigils, called *Virgulta Divina*. It is likely meant to be *Virgula Divina* which is Latin for "divine stick" (or "divining rod"). It is to be made of brass or copper, it is V-shaped, and there are numerous sigils including those of the moon nodes, and at each end is a pentagram, square, and triangle.

---

16 De Laurence Co., 1919.

17 See *Speculum Terrae: A Magical Earth Mirror From The 17th Century*, by Frater Acher, Hadean Press, 2018: "Whether supported by a wooden enclosure or crafted entirely from cardboard—even despite the fact that they would have been confiscated and destroyed by the authorities upon discovery—earth mirrors themselves present incredibly fragile objects ... They existed, at least most known cases, to fulfill a rather worldly function by use of magical means—and that was to discover hidden treasures in forests, fields and caves."

Invocations are included, calling upon Jesus Christ and the various Hebrew names of God, and also the choirs or "Orders of Angels". Also mentioned is Henry Cornelius Agrippa, and the text obviously draws from the *Three Books of Occult Philosophy*, specifically naming the various archangels, including Metatron and others; additionally, there are the angels ruling over the signs of the zodiac, which are also noted in the later book *The Magus, or Celestial Intelligencer* by Francis Barrett, 1801, the text of which was based on (if not plagiarized from) Agrippa's work.

There are pages with twenty-one planetary talismanic sigils including the intelligences and demons of each of the seven planets, that are also found in *Three Books of Occult Philosophy* by Agrippa, as well as in *The Key of Solomon the King*, and *The Magus* by Barrett.[18] Additionally, there are angels of the days of the week, as well as the individual spirit or "angel of the air" for each day of the week, along with specific incense for each.

As noted above, the text mentions specific spirits related to the *Goetia* and *Abramelin*, called "the orders of the hellish spirits", including Asmodeus, Belial, and Astaroth, as well as demonic spirits from both Hebrew and Christian sources, such as Beelzebub, Abaddon, and others from various traditions. Also, "the torments of the damned", based on the Hebrew Qliphoth, on the "rivers of hell" and the "princes of hell", and more.

Lastly, there are instructions for the creation of the "Staff of Caroli", which is necessary to use in the final portions of the invocation to acquire hidden treasure. It is used for protection from the spirits, and to compel them to release the treasure and to help move it from one place to another.

Regarding the one guarding the treasure, they are referred to simply as a "poor soul" who is being tortured by wicked spirits, but these are not named as being *Mouras* or gnomes, or even as "terrestrial spirits", such as in other works. The spirits are

---

18 See bibliography.

commanded to pack up the treasure from their lair, and then to deliver it to the operator, by the power of the name of Jesus Christ. It is mentioned in *Le Petit Albert*, "When we have solid reasons to believe (it is) the spirits of dead men who guard the treasures, it is good to have blessed candles, instead of common candles; and to conjure them from God, to declare whether we can do something to put them in a good place of rest. We must never fail to carry out what has been asked for."

I have to confess that it is truly a pleasure for a grimoire enthusiast such as myself to discover such a treasure as this little text, and to be able to translate and present it to the general public for the first time. There are dozens of new translations of established grimoire titles on the book market today, but it is rare to find one that has not yet been discovered and translated into the English language. I can certainly see how it would have been easy to pass over a relatively brief section of a large compilation entitled simply *Pneumatologia Occulta et Vera*, but as it unexpectedly (and pleasantly surprisingly) turns out, it is quite a little diamond in the rough.

Morals

HISTORICAL INTRODUCTION TO THIS WRITING.[19]

First Part

I FEEL MYSELF obligated to communicate the "Pneumatologia Occulta" completely to my readers. I will only give historical notes and short extracts from the other writings of this kind. A complete historical note[20] however, which illustrates modern theurgy to the historian, belongs in the Magic Library according to its scientific tendency. Since the "Pneumatologia" is now valued very highly and has not yet been printed, so I considered it most appropriate.

The whole of the immediately preceding essay on theurgy[21] is intended as an introduction to the various theurgical writings of which the Magic Library will give information. Whoever reads these carefully will find themselves in a position to judge such writings from the right point of view.

It is not at all necessary that we utter an ecclesiastical-Orthodox curse[22] on them, as happens with the older books on magic, or even accuse them of blasphemy. This would appear in our times only as a ridiculous zeal, and rightly itself to be laughed at. The heartbreaking theurgical prayer[23] at the beginning of

---

19 Translator's note: "Schrift", writing or scripture. This opening essay was written by Georg Conrad Horst, introducing the text of "Pneumatologia Occulta" in *Zauber-Bibliothek* (*The Magic Library*), volume one, 1821.

20 Translator's note: "historische Notizen".

21 Translator's note: The previous section of *Zauber-Bibliothek* is entitled "Iamblich. ein großer Verehrer der theurgißchen Wissenschaften. Deßen Ansichten vom Geißterreich, der Magie, und Theurgie." (Iamblichus. Great admirer of the theurgical sciences. His opinions on the kingdom of spirits, magic, and theurgy).

22 Translator's note: "kirchlich-orthodoxe Bannfluche".

23 Translator's note: "herzbrechende theurgische Gebet".

the "Pneumatologia Occulta" is, however, in a certain sense a misuse of the name of God. It is not communicated as a model of a reasonable, godly prayer, but as a historical contribution to theurgy in modern times. No history can be written without such acts. Theurgy, however, is an essential part of history both in the old [world] and in the new.

Of the intelligent reader, [this] will cause them to reflect seriously on the various aberrations[24] of the human mind, and that is enough. Others will laugh at it, and that doesn't hurt either. It cannot be dangerous to anyone who has understanding (the ignorant can misuse the Bible, and—abuse it!) or lead him to superstition, this is the main thing.

However, there may still be a few moral and religious statements by older and more recent thinkers about the content and tendency of such writings. In order not to write a new treatise, we transcribe it here without a commentary. For the discerning person, the material is provided for further reflection. The less insightful or inquisitive can use it as a lesson and warning, which I hereby also urge, with regard to inquisitive theurgic arts, to read the most wondrous and indeed terrifying stories that they have written in this part of the *Zauber-Bibliothek* (volume IV), in which an incident is reported that has not yet been clarified historically.[25]

In addition, the various passages that we want to mention can at the same time shed a closer light on individual points in the preceding essay from a scientific point of view.

---

24 Translator's note: "mannichfachen Verirrungen".

25 Translator's note: There are various Faustian legends presented in volume four of *Zauber-Bibliothek*, including reference to the infamous *Miracle* book (volume IV, page 123), also known as the *Threefold Coercion of Hell* or the *Black Raven*, which is what I assume Horst may be referring to here.

II

It becomes all too diverse in tense expectation[26], often betrayed in the theurgy of deceit and trickery. It cannot be explained at all how the gods and demons should allow themselves to be commanded by weaker people, as soon as they please to speak to them. They demand that whoever wants to serve them must be more just. But they give themselves up to carry out unjust acts as soon as the theurge ordered them to do so? This is a contradiction that confuses me (Porphyry).[27]

In which case can a dangerous deception take place in the appearance of gods and demons?

When something has been provided in the theurgical art, and instead of the required true appearances, others come to light. In this case the lower and imperfect spirits easily take the form of the higher ones. In this way, a multitude of great and dangerous errors often arise in the citation of spirits. Whoever trusts such false appearances will be plunged into delusions, and led away from the true knowledge of God. Because why do they appear? Something to give an advantage to those who cite it? No, to deceive them and to harm them! Because no benefit can be expected from the lie. Divine nature as the eternal source of being and truth does not allow exchanging the image of itself to pass into any other object (Iamblic.).[28]

---

26 Translator's note: "vielfältig wird die allzu gespannte".

27 Original footnote: In the previous essay on angelic letters. So even these people were judged more roughly than their system at sober moments, and (they) drew attention to the possible negative consequences of their enthusiasm ("Schwärmereien", passion). Translator's note: Porphyry of Tyre (c. 234–c. 305 CE) was a Tyrian Neoplatonic philosopher, born in Tyre or Syria during Roman rule. He edited and published the *Enneads*, the only known collection of work attributed to his teacher Plotinus.

28 Original footnote: *De Mysteriis Aegypt.* II.c. 10. Translator's note: Iamblichus (c. 245–c. 325 CE) was a Syrian Neoplatonist philosopher of Arab origin. He determined the direction that would later be taken by Neoplatonic philosophy.

The highest commandment in the art of the spirit—theurgy—is that one should know what he should ask, and accept from the spirits for his use, or [what] not to accept. As was Midas then, this is the best example which, since he wanted to turn all things into gold, he attracted such a spirit that could do such things. But this wicked spirit deceived him so much, that if the mercy of God had not improved his folly, he must certainly have died of hunger. Therefore, people contemplated the right commandment of the spirit art, and the stories of Midas, like old histories, [people] did not believe they were fictitious fables.[29] They would be more careful in their appeals to the spirits; and therefore they would not be exterminated by [those who are] not spiritual, while they strive to reach the golden mountain from the lowest [place][30] (*Clavicula Salomonis*).[31]

He was also the biographer of the Greek mystic, philosopher and mathematician Pythagoras. See *Iamblichus; De Mysteriis Aegyptiorum, Chaldaeorum, Assyriorum*, Venice: Aldus Manutius, 1497, translation by Marsilio Ficino; also, *Iamblichus on the Mysteries of the Egyptians, Chaldeans, and Assyrians*, translation by Thomas Taylor, Wizards Bookshelf, 1997.

29 Translator's note: See *Three Books of Occult Philosophy* by Henry Cornelius Agrippa, editor Donald Tyson, Llewelyn Publishing, 1993/2019. On page 602, it states: "Midas—The wealthy and effeminate king of Phrygia, who was said to have been given the gift by Silenus of turning everything he touched into gold. When he discovered that he could not eat, he begged Silenus to remove the gift. Silenus told him to bathe in the spring that was the source of the river Pactolus, which cleansed Midas of the curse, and turned the river sands golden."

30 Translator's note: "zum güldenen Berge von niedersten zu gelangen trachten".

31 Original footnote: This is how even this scripture, which defends magic and theurgy, expresses itself and draws attention to the dangers of the theurgical guild ("theurgischer Zünfte"). Translator's note: The "Key of Solomon" or "Greater Key", which is one of the most popular texts of ceremonial magic. The first English edition was transcribed by S.L. MacGregor Mathers, and published in London by George Redway, 1889. There are numerous references to gold in the "Key of Solomon", most notably the preparation of gold used to construct pentacles/talismans of the Sun. It was based on classic manuscripts, as well as being widely quoted in the popular text by Heinrich Cornelius Agrippa von Nettesheim (1486–1535), who was a German physician, theologian, and

The true and divine magic consists primarily in the right, true worship, and teaches you to know the creator and the creature; [it] instructs us in the divine secrets incomprehensible to natural man, tells us future things, opens up contact with the *mundo intelligentiarum*[32] or the angels and spirits. It teaches us to do miraculous things, opens the heart of nature for us, and gives us a foretaste[33] of the future, eternal joy and glory.

But superstitious magic has nothing in common with *magia vera*[34] except for the divine names, which it shamefully misuses. [It] should really not be called *magia* because it is full of superstition, and the assistance of fallen or deceptive spirits.[35] Because woe to the person whose soul turns away from the true spirit of magic, and turns to the elements. Anyone who knows that evil spirits can also transform themselves into angels of light will refrain from all presumption, and try nothing but to glorify the great name of God (von Eckartshausen, from an oriental manuscript).[36]

The human mind, of course, has a tendency to explore the supersensible,[37] because the finite cannot satisfy it. But that is why the view beyond the world of the senses is not yet an insight into the world of spirits; and only an intoxicated mind can imagine that it will find a higher knowledge beyond the limits of the

---

occult writer. His popular *Three Books of Occult Philosophy*, published in 1533, drew heavily upon Kabbalah, Hermeticism, and Neoplatonism. His book was widely influential among occultists of the early modern period, and was condemned as heretical by the inquisitor of Cologne.

32 Translator's note: Latin for "the world of intelligences".

33 Translator's note: "Vorgeschmack ".

34 Translator's note: Latin for "true magic".

35 Translator's note: "hulfleistung abgefallener oder tauschender Geister ist".

36 Translator's note: Karl von Eckartshausen (28 June 1752–12 May 1803) was a German Catholic mystic, author, and philosopher. See *Magic: The Principles of Higher Knowledge* (translated into English and edited by Gerhard Hanswille & Deborah Brumlich, Merkur Publishing, 1989).

37 Translator's note: "uebersinnlichen", supernatural.

knowable. However, if the human understanding nevertheless wants to penetrate the realm of the supersensible, nothing else is left to it than to transform concepts into real beings, and to identify perceptions with what is seen. From this arises a theurgic philosophy, or similar to the Alexandrian philosophy, and reason is utterly shipwrecked[38] (Tennemann).[39]

We do not doubt for a moment that the various classes of our readers will put everything in its right place in the following manuscript; and will appreciate reason all the more when reading it, the more [that] one can preserve its light, which alone is able to protect [them] from enthusiasm and superstition. This requires magic and theurgy in the labyrinth spaces in order to find one's way around them with certainty, and to preserve the spirit's freedom and independence.

And now just a few more historical words about our "Pneumatologia Occulta".

Second Part

The name "Salamancan" Pneumatologia Occulta could seem ominous, in that we do not expect any particular information either about the spirit realm or any other branch of human knowledge from the University of Salamanca. The foreword of the manuscript explains quite simply that the "Pneumatologia Occulta" was publicly taught at Salamanca in his day. In this connection I must remark that the "Pneumatologia Occulta" was still being read at Protestant universities in the first half of the last century, especially at Halle, where my eternal father (from which professor I can no longer remember) heard it himself in the

---

38 Translator's note: "Schiffbruch".

39 Translator's note: Wilhelm Gottlieb Tennemann (7 December 1761–30 September 1819) was a German historian of philosophy.

thirties, as I can still remember from his story.[40]

Otherwise one could think of the so-called devil's school or the devil's college,[41] a university building in Salamanca that bears this name. This devil's college is noted in I.A. Ballenstedt's essay on some oddities of the lands of Brunswick[42] (1771). To prove how much our good ancestors tampered with the devil, this scholar occasionally mentions an astonishing number of names in Brunswick, which are put together with that of his hellish majesty; for example, the Teufelsbald, the devil's leap, etc., where occasionally the devil's school at Salamanca is also mentioned. Professor Fischer in his *Flying Pages*[43] St. III. S. 364. believes that this building perhaps got its name because the burning of the alleged devils and witches, as one puts it, was taught therein, since nowhere, as is known, were so many witches burned as in Spain.

There is, however, another, more obvious reason for the name, which is conspicuous for a public school building, at least presumably, which is too funny and entertaining for us not to give to our readers in this introduction; and perhaps the matter is really historically related to the report of our manuscript in Salamanca. Here is the adventurous tale, so characteristic of the story of magic, that for this very reason it deserves to be quoted!

---

40 Translator's note: Martin Luther University of Halle-Wittenberg, referred to as MLU, a public, research-oriented university in the cities of Halle and Wittenberg in the State of Saxony-Anhalt, Germany. The university was created in 1817 through the merger of the University of Wittenberg (founded in 1502) and the University of Halle (founded in 1694). The university is named after the Protestant reformer Martin Luther, who was a professor in Wittenberg.

41 Translator's note: "Teufelscollegiums".

42 Translator's note: "Braunschweigischen Länder».

43 Translator's note: *Fliegende Blätter* or '*Flying Pages*' was a German satirical magazine published in Munich from 1845–1944; however it is uncertain if this refers to that publication.

II

When, long years ago, the devil, in visible form as a magister or private docent, publicly taught the black art at the high school in Salamanca in Spain, in an underground vault of a university building there, at the end of his lectures he quite unexpectedly required, instead of an honorarium, the soul of one of the audience who was chosen by lot to be the last to exit the college. The unfortunate number fell to a young count of Almeida.[44] This courageous young man, however, by a strange ruse, managed to escape the clutches of the villain. The terrible supreme master of all black artisans lurked at the door at the top of the stairs for him. The count, who then knew that the devil was a man of his word, yes, a true slave of his word, had meanwhile devised a ruse; and confidently walked towards his fate, trusting that it would be a success. On the top step of the stairs, the murderous spirit roared at him in a terrifying voice: Stop, fellow! that I may break your neck! It was just at noon when the group of students was leaving, and the sun was directly opposite the entrance to the building. "What do you want?", answered the count very calmly. "I am not the last, hold on to the one who follows me," and pointed with his hand to his own shadow. Immediately Satan disappeared and let the mischievous student go out free. From that moment on, however, the count's body never again cast a shadow in the sunshine, as an obvious proof that the devil must really have taken it to hell with him (Musäus Strausfedern B. I. Num. IV. S. 197. f.).

And now immediately to our manuscript, which we finally provide—with the omission of a few insignificant passages—with great care taken of its orthography, punctuation, etc., just as it is, without essential changes, placed here in front of us.[45]

---

44 Translator's note: "die unglückliche Nummer traf einen jungen Grafen von Almeida".

45 Original footnote: foreword and notes from Horst, *Zauber-Bibliothek*, Volume I, 1821.

The Hidden and True
Pneumatology

Preface

In Nomine ter Sancti Seph.[46]
To the willing reader.

IT IS UNDENIABLE that at Salamanca in Spain[47] about 180 years ago, the hidden teaching of the spirits[48] was still presented in secret, whereas it was public previously; as I myself then saw one and

---

46 Translator's note: Latin, "In the name of Saint Seph", possibly meaning Saint Joseph or Saint Seth.

47 Original footnote: One must bear in mind that, in the Middle Ages, Spain was generally notorious as a real magical land, to which the presence of the Saracens contributed much that was accused of Satanism and Manichaeism. And so it appears also in the excellent old folk book, of Fortunatus and his satchel and wishing-hat. Quite diverting to read etc., Augspurg, 1530, of which Gorres (Teutsche Volksb. 74.) has shown that it has been translated from Spanish, the following passage, which is of interest to our conjecture: "Fortunatus said: Is the master who made it still alive? The king said, I don't know that, it (was) one from Sparga (Spain) in the city of Alamanelia, where there is still the school of the high art of Nigromantia, and [who] had been taught there as a great, well-learned Doctor of Nigromantia." Comp. *Fortunatus* etc. From the English, by F.W.V. Schmidt (Berlin, 1819.) p. 212.

Translator's notes: Saracen was a term used by Christian writers in Europe during the Middle Ages to refer to Muslims, primarily of Arab origin, but also those of Turkic and Persian/Iranian origins. Manichaeism is a dualistic religious system with Christian, Gnostic, and pagan elements, founded in Persia in the third century by Manes (c. 216–c. 276). The system was based on a supposed primeval conflict between light and darkness. It spread widely in the Roman Empire and in Asia and survived in eastern Turkestan (Xinjiang) until the thirteenth century. *Fortunatus* is a German proto-novel or chapbook about a legendary hero, popular in fifteenth and sixteenth centuries in Europe and usually associated with a magical inexhaustible purse.

48 Translator's note: "verborgene Geister Lehre".

another manuscript in certain libraries, and therein found special ways, how the good spirits may be retained, but the harmful ones [are] expelled by divine approval.

Just as this is the basic principle of the present treatise, the whole proof is based on the only religion; and all those miracles that happen in the temple in Jerusalem can be deduced from this reason, if we would not distort the whole book of the Holy Bible.

But there can be no practice of religion unless a good demon[49] is involved.

But whether such a good spirit[50] may be drawn to us in different ways; so we earthly people are nevertheless unable to bind them.

Because the better and the more pure such a being is, the closer it comes to the being of the Creator, who is absolute.

Nevertheless, it is not impossible to incite such spirits through certain incantations, so that they come closer to us.

This the old paganism[51], which as much in the true world-wisdom as in the knowledge of the creator[52] and nature was not inexperienced, understood only too well.

To cite only one and another example, we read in Apuleius,[53] how he willed to himself such spirits through the stars in heaven; through the sub-spirits; through all natural elements; through the nightly silence; through the growth of the Nile streams;[54] through Memphite secrets, and the like.

And in Porphyry it is stated: You who were brought out of the dust; who sits in your place and sails on the sea; who changes your shape every hour; and are transformed by all; and so on.

---

49 Translator's note: "guter Daemon".

50 Translator's note: "guter Geist ".

51 Translator's note: "Heydenthum".

52 Translator's note: "Schöpfers".

53 Translator's note: Apuleius was a Numidian Latin-language prose writer, Platonist philosopher and rhetorician.

54 Translator's note: "Nil-strohms".

By invocations of this kind, which are nothing [other] than signs of the hidden properties, the ancients have indeed found that such spirits put themselves at the service of men; not by compulsion, but voluntarily; because they are free creatures who are free from them, and [they] like to deal with pure people.

The greatest however, is the communion of the deity, of which the human mind plays a part; hence these spirits impart their powers and qualities voluntarily.

From this source all illuminations, prophecies, dreams, miracles and the like do flow, in that these good spirits, because we are like them in essence according to the infused immortal spirit, work in and with us; on the contrary, the wicked spirits, with the help of these good ones, are driven away from us; which cannot happen if man does not seek to unite with the good spirits.[55]

So just as an exorcist thus makes the invocations through the divine powers; through the sacred names or supernatural qualities; through the most sacred secrets and sacraments, making an earthly-minded heart tremble; so the spirits who have fallen away from God may just as little stand before it. Because of this, Cyprianus[56] says in *Libro: Quod idola Dii non sint*:[57] that such spirits, when they are invoked by the true God, themselves confess that they yield from the possessed bodies, so must leave immediately; and either rise up at once, or gradually lose their power in such bodies after the faith of the possessed ones is procured; or by the grace of God, the conjurer has greater powers.

---

55 Translator's note: "mit den guten Geistern zu vereinigen trachtet".

56 Translator's note: Saint Cyprian (third century?–304 CE), supposed author of the famous grimoire text "Book of St Cyprian", known by the title "the Magician" to distinguish him from Cyprian, Bishop of Carthage, received a liberal education in his youth, and particularly applied himself to astrology, after which he traveled for improvement through Greece, Egypt, India, etc. Cyprian was described as a magician in Antioch and said to have dealt in sorcery.

57 Translator's note: Latin, "in the book: *That the Idols Are Not Gods*".

And Athanasius[58] in the book *de Variis Quaest*[59], writes that there is no word more terrifying to such unclean spirits, and which weakens their strength more, than the beginning of the 68th Psalm. May God rise up, so that his enemies are scattered before him, and those who hate him will flee;[60] as soon as these words are uttered, the devil must leave.

Origen's *Contra Celsum*[61] also reports that by naming Jesus, as experience shows, countless devils[62] were driven away from the human body.

But because one may not want to agree with these statements of one and another church fathers, so I will cite some heathen[63] for several proofs, who knew from experience, that the power of words against unclean spirits will have a great effect.

That sorceress in Lucan says:[64]

---

58 Translator's note: Probably referring to Athanasius I of Alexandria (c. 296/298–2 May 373), also called Athanasius the Great, Athanasius the Confessor or, primarily in the Coptic Orthodox Church, Athanasius the Apostolic, who was a Greek church father and the twentieth bishop of Alexandria. He was exiled repeatedly, when he was replaced on the order of four different Roman emperors. He was a Christian theologian, the chief defender of Trinitarianism against Arianism, and a noted Coptic Christian (Egyptian) leader of the fourth century.

59 Translator's note: Latin, "On a Variety of Questions".

60 Translator's note: The first passage of Psalm 68 from the King James Bible: "Let God arise, let his enemies be scattered: let them also that hate him flee before him."

61 Translator's note: The *Contra Celsum* is the culmination of the great apologetic movement of the second and third centuries CE and is for the Greek Church what St Augustine's *City of God* is for Western Christendom. It is also one of the chief monuments of the coming together of ancient Greek culture and the new faith of the expanding Christian society.

62 Translator's note: "unzählige Teufel".

63 Translator's note: "Heyden", pagan.

64 Translator's note: "jene Zauberin beym Lucano saget", i.e. in book VI of the *Pharsalia*.

jam vos ego nomine vero eliciam, Stygiosque canes[65] in luce superna destituam per busta sequar, per funera Custos Expellam tumulis, abigam vos omnibus Vrnis, te que Deis, ad quos alio procedere Vultu, Ficta Soles, Hecate...

That is:

I will draw you out by the true name, so that you hellhounds have no more power in the upper light; I will pursue you through the graves, and as a protector of the corpses I will chase you away from them and from all the urns of the dead, and you Hecate, who turn to the gods with a disguised face, I will present you to them in your pale form and hinder you, that you may no longer change your hellish countenance.[66]

I find another testimony from Philostratus,[67] who cites the example of Apollonius and his companions, with whom he traveled over land in the bright moonlight.

---

65 Translator's note: In Greek mythology, Cerberus (or Kérberos) is described as the "Hound of Hades", and usually depicted as a three-headed dog with a serpent tail, who guards the gates of the Underworld to prevent the dead from leaving. He was described as being the offspring of the monsters Echidna and Typhon.

66 Translator's note: "ich werde euch in dem wahren Nahmen hervor ziehen, das ihr Hollenhunde in dem obern Licht keine Gewalt mehr habet; ich werde euch durch die Graber verfolgen, und als eine Beschutzerin der Leichen von selbigen und von allen Todten Topfen verjagen, und du Hecate, die du dich mit verstelltem Gesicht zu den Gottern wendest, dich will ich ihnen in deiner blasen Gestalt darstellen und verhinderen, das du dein hollisches Angesicht nicht mehr verwandten konnest."

67 Translator's note: Philostratus, or Lucius Flavius Philostratus (c. 170 – 247/250 CE), who was known as "the Athenian", and was a Greek sophist of the Roman imperial period. His father was a minor sophist of the same name. He was probably born around 170 and is said by the *Suda* to have been living in the reign of emperor Philip the Arab (244–249). He died probably in Tyre about 250 CE. There are also several others by this name.

These (travelers) met a ghost, which changed its shape without stopping, and entertained their eyes.

As soon as Apollonius saw it, he addressed it with threatening words. He encouraged his traveling companions to do the same, whereupon the ghost disappeared before their eyes.

For this kind of spirit is very fearful when the human being knows how to properly use the divine properties communicated to him.

But so I do not go too far in my words, but rather do enough for the reader [to understand], one must know what the true golden chain of Homer[68] is, namely the connection of all creatures from which the bonds of such unclean spirits must be brought forth.[69][70]

These are of three kinds; one of these is taken from the elementary world, when we conjure up a spirit through things that are below us, the powers of which he knows, and are pleasant or contrary to him; and either want to lure him to us, or to drive him away from us.

This takes place through the whole of Egyptian wisdom and all its hieroglyphic symbols, through blood, through flowers, through herbs and animals, through the elements, and the like. (As still used in the Roman Church, at the consecration of the

---

68 Translator's note: "wahre Kuldene Kette des Homeri".

69 Translator's note: "die Bänder solcher unreinen Geister musen hergeholet werden".

70 Translator's note: Anton Kirchweger (died 8 February 1746) was the editor or the author of the influential hermetic text *Aurea Catena Homeri* (Golden Chain of Homer), full title Aurea Catena Homeri oder, Eine Beschreibung von dem Ursprung der Natur und natürlichen Dingen (The Golden Chain of Homer, or A Description of the Origin of Nature and Natural Things). The book was read by Pietists and later influenced the young Goethe. It was first published in Leipzig in 1723, in the German language, followed by other editions: 1723, 1728, 1738 and 1757 (Latin edition). Another Latin version was issued at Frankfurt in 1762. Sometime in the late eighteenth century Sigismund Bacstrom translated parts of the work into English. In 1891, part of the translation was published in the Theosophical Society journal *Lucifer*.

baptism of water, on the evening of the holy Three Kings,[71] at the consecration of the Easter candles and otherwise, special names are used in their consecration.) The reason lies in this antipathy and sympathy of the spirits with the signature of such things attracted, with which they either have a fellowship, or have a disgust for it.

The other bond is taken from the firmament, when we invoke the spirits of the sky, of the stars, through their movement, rays, light, clarity, power, influences, and so on.

This bond is rooted in such spirits in the manner of an admonition; or also in response to an order to such service-spirits,[72] which are of the lowest sort.

The third bond, as the strongest, is received from God and through God; and can only be carried out through true religion.

Here we invoke the spirits through the Divine Name itself,[73] through the divine powers, through the seals and secrets of religion, through the sacraments and that which goes with them.

This bond entails an actual command, and is precisely the one which the Most Holy Cabbala, and the pure Rabbinic Schemhamphoras,[74] through which Moses and other prophets practiced all things incomprehensible to reason.

Here, however, it should be noted that there is a general and special providence, so [there are] also special spirits and powers under the general spirit of the world.

Hence such evocators initially make use of the uppermost bonds, through their names and invocation of their forces, that rule everything below them. This is how, through these bonds, not only the spirits themselves are inhibited, but also the other

---

71 Translator's note: i.e., Epiphany.

72 Translator's note: "Dienstgeister".

73 Translator's note: "Göttlichen Nahmen selbst".

74 Translator's note: The secret or hidden name of God in both Judaism and occultism. Shem HaMephorash literally means "the explicit name". This describes a hidden name of God in Kabbalah, and is composed of either 4, 12, 22, 42, or 72 letters, the name of 72 being the most common.

creatures and effects of nature which are subject to them; for example, thunderstorms, bursts of fire, breaks in clouds, floods, pestilence, diseases, violence of weapons, harm to animals, and so on. This happens, among other things, with the invocation of serpents, since in addition to the divine name and all natural forces, the secret mysteries of religion are also mixed in; for example, the curse of the serpent in the earthly paradise, the erection of the serpent in the desert[75] and the words of the 91st Psalm, upon lions and adders you will tread and step upon the young lions and dragons.[76]

Incidentally, it is certain that through this true divine wisdom we can perform in nature all those miracles which our ancestors performed in true faith.

It is also to be admired that the clergy of our church, in which true faith is supposed, do not use the spiritual magic rod[77], [perhaps] to test whether the spirits are subservient, and the rest of nature shows obedience to them.

Incidentally, one recognizes that the spirits, along with the divine, may also be driven out by natural means.

David himself would not have made effective use of his harp against the force of the evil spirit,[78] if he had not observed this

---

[75] Translator's note: There are a few possible Bible passages in this regard; for example, John 3:14, "And as Moses lifted up the serpent in the wilderness, so must the Son of Man be lifted up", and Numbers 21:9, "So Moses made a bronze serpent and set it on a pole. And if a serpent bit anyone, he would look at the bronze serpent and live."

[76] Translator's note: Passage 13 of Psalm 91 in the King James Bible: "Thou shalt tread upon the lion and adder: the young lion and the dragon shalt thou trample under feet."

[77] Translator's note: The "divine rod" or "divining rod" described later in this text.

[78] Translator's note: 1 Samuel 16:14–23. David's playing on his harp was the only thing that would settle King Saul's troubled mind. When an evil spirit from God came upon King Saul, David would take his harp and play and King Saul would feel better, and the evil spirit would leave him.

order by initially calling upon the name of the Most High, as a man after the heart of God, which he did because he wanted to kill the giant Goliath, and said:

The Lord who saves me from the lion and the bear, will also save me from this Philistine.[79]

Thereupon he came forth to him, not according to the powers of his nature, but by the power of his divine magic, in the name of the Lord Zebaoth, the God of the hosts of Israel; in whose name he felled this dangerous opponent, etc.

End of the preface to the willing reader.

---

[79] Translator's note: The Philistines were an ancient people who lived on the south coast of Canaan from the 12th century BCE until 604 BCE, when their polity, after having already been subjugated for centuries by the Neo-Assyrian Empire, was finally destroyed by King Nebuchadnezzar II of the Neo-Babylonian Empire. We all know of the famous tale of David and Goliath; See 1 Samuel.

Prayer[80]

LORD, HOLY AND TRUE God Zebaoth![81] How holy, holy is the clarity of your wonderful name! How glorious and worshipful, how majestic and marvelous, is the Most Holy Name of God to my soul! The name of Jehovah, in which the Holy Trinity is and has its throne; it is too majestic for me, because of its holiness. My soul trembles at the same time, when this holy name resounds in my ears! Call out with the cherubim and seraphim, who cover their faces and hide them from the sanctity of this wonderful name, saying: Holy! Holy! Holy! is the name of the Lord of hosts, the name of Jesus Jehovah! Oh, that my soul might melt away in the praise of this holy, holy, holy highly-blessed name of God. Holy! Holy! Holy! to me is the dearly blessed and dearly loved name of Jesus! To me He is the scent of life unto life! I find in it an open door, which I can enter into the heart of the eternal, dear father. The holy balsam smell of this refreshes and permeates all my limbs! It passes through all my joints and all my veins as a balm! It is my treasure. I have chosen it for myself, I want to keep it for my own; and as a headdress; and as a sash to tie around my head. The holy name of Jesus should be a safe defense and a fortified castle for me, where I can flee from my enemies at all times; so that my enemy does not catch me, that the power of Belial cannot touch my soul! When this holy name of the Holy Trinity reveals itself to me, then everything is light. The shining of fatherly love, and the

---

80 Translator's note: It is common practice with Christian grimoires, such as the *Enchiridion of Pope Leo III* (see *Crossed Keys* by Michael Ceccetelli, Scarlet Imprint, 2010), to open with a lengthy Catholic prayer.

81 Translator's note: "Herr, Heiliger und Warhaftiger Gott Zebaoth!" (or "God of Hosts"). The word Zebaoth (in Hebrew צבאות), or Sabaoth or Tzevaot, is a name of God in the Hebrew tradition, meaning "the hosts of heaven", as in the biblical title "Lord (God) of Sabaoth". It is used numerous times in this text. See Appendix A.

essential light of the word, and the pure flame of the spirit with its sevenfold power of light, then all at once reveal themselves in my innermost chamber; and it blows out from the father of love when he reveals to me this, his grace-blessed loving name, his true peace. My soul rests in great pride; my spirit is blessed; my heart demands nothing else, when it is surrounded and immersed in this; in this holy miracle the name of the Lord my God.

Oh you wonderful heart-, soul- and spirit-refreshing beloved name! That you might so openly reveal yourself to all your children; and to all those who genuinely desire to be born again in your fatherly heart! Then, when I have your essential strength, I don't want anything [else]. I can confidently rely on this sacred name, and not be afraid; even if a thousand are on my side, and tens of thousands are around me on my left, waiting to storm in.

This name is a banner over my head, a covering over my right hand, and a roof from the heat of the world's troubles and temptation. It is a safe refuge for me, when my ship is almost covered by the waves, so that it does not perish.

He is my living anchor, my eternal green and blooming rock; who neither gives way nor wavers, my refuge. He is the rock of my honor, I hope in him and I will be helped.

He is my consolation in troubled times; this name shall be my ruler; I want nothing but this name; I do not ask for any other bliss, for alone is the name of the Lord of hosts, of the mighty Jehovah! When I have and possess this holy name, the name of Jesus, I have everything; even if I have no other goods on earth, no gifts, no spiritual treasures; then this name is everything! I have fallen in love with him. He is the bridegroom of my soul, the savior of my wounded heart. He is my refuge and my protector. He is my Redeemer and my strong David; He is my hero in battle; He is my mighty victorious prince. He overcomes death in me. He led me to steadily die; and in him, he also brought me further and further to a holy new life. When I have written this living name, alive in my soul and on my forehead, nothing can happen to me: nothing can break me; I cannot lose anything. But if I am lacking and break this sacred name, what do I have then, when I have all the possessions in the whole world? When have I been able and possess all the gifts of grace and all spiritual gifts? Without this holy name, which is an eternal holy name, then I cannot live.

You, the three times holy, holy, holy, deserve the honor of worship! You deserve prizes of power, splendor, strength and honor, majesty, victory and conquest! All of the ardent love from your creatures is due to your eternal fatherly heart, that is full of compassion! Of your most glorious holy name, which alone works miracles, deserves honor and adoration forever! Your majesty, your glorious kingdom, and you, the ruler of all, you deserve my adoration, your most sacred and eternal love deserves the most reliable and willing obedience of love! Your eternal, living, fatherly heart flowing with love, which has presented itself as a bread of strength, it is brought forth well, it deserves a complete sacrifice and dedication of all inner and outer powers of the whole will and desire of spirit! Your love, which is compassionate to all their works, your eyes are on me due to my infinite humble gratitude! Your eternal wisdom, which your people can draw up in every net, it is due glory! All glory is due to your power of redemption that brings the end! You are the omnipotent God of hosts! Most invincible, most powerful monarch! You are the ultimate source of all created things! Your origin and source, into which all creatures must flow; take in poor life and the babbling of a sluggish sound, which in this hour you have blown upon with the breath of your sanctuary! You are praised, O father! before the revelation of your fatherly love; so that your people now have joyful access through Jesus Christ into your fatherly heart! You are praised, Oh Lord, because of the revelation of your thrice-holy, miraculous name, which is called Lord Zebaoth; that now a soul which is attacked by the bird of prey can find eternal refuge! Lord be praised. You are the hero in the controversy, before your gracious revelation of the eternal inheritance that you promised your children; and you have chosen them to own it; that now, after they have been made completely naked and bare by the temptation, they come back to you, eternal one, rich and full of grace, [that they] may take of your grace! You are to be praised, powerfully commanding me before your grace; that we can recognize you as you are, and what your hand demands of us; that we again become your image; and into your eternal quiet serenity can be incorporated! Be praised for your wonderful communication of your powerful word, which you present to every starving heart; and speak it to him, that he can have life and be full of satisfaction! Your fatherly heart must be praised and blessed; because of your kindness, your enemies find mercy; and their misery, so they turn to you, you let be removed from them; that you now make a fountain again all uncleanness[82] and so filled from the source of your love, you can also forgive your enemies! You are to be praised before your wisdom, by which your poor heir can pass through all trials and temptations, and pass through so they will not perish again, but under your hand, under the shadow of your banner, can safely walk the narrow path to completion, to haven and treasure which you have placed in them! Your eternal hand of strength must be praised and adored; and which will soon bring the end of all things! Hallelujah! Glory be to you, oh God! and ever forever! everything that lives, praise the name of the Lord! All islands and all mountains resound! All fountains rise up! Every valley ring out! All the streams, the brooks and lakes roar in praise of the name of the omnipotent ruler of the land, who now sits on his holy throne, and shall sit upon the earth!

---

82 Translator's note: "Born", wellspring; see Isa. 12:3.

There he will establish the fortress of his throne, which is deep in the hearts of his loved ones; and they will sacrifice to him day by day and month by month; holy sacrifices to praise his name as forever chosen by him; to honor kings and priests in holy adornments. Oh ruler and duke of life! Glory be your name without end. Your glory will be spread out in little time, from one end of the earth to the other. Everything, everything, everything will be full. It will be full of your glory; and you have thought of your people; you have set out to visit them with salvation and grace. Hallelujah! Sing to him, you cherubim and seraphim! Then the day of the wedding of the lamb is before the door; and his bride is prepared, and ready to be presented to her husband as an adorned maiden, blameless and unsullied. Yes, Oh Holy One! What praise and jubilation will go up to you when the sabbath begins, from the lower choirs! They will fill all the thrones with praise! The wine of your loving spirit will roar, and make them drunk, that they shout Victory! Our king lives! one after the other; and with this king who loved them so dearly and brought them to his likeness, they will rule from one eternity to another. Hallelujah! Call all the creatures, that the savior comes! Praise him before his Holy Word, which he has promised to make clear; and makes you noble from out of your madness and rudeness! Praise him all his holy angels, who are ready day and night to surround the people of the Lord and to keep and maintain them. Those who always diligently establish the word and the will of Jehovah! Praise him, as all are as the perfect first fruits, or [those] who have already entered into the rest and joy of your Lord. Then also [those] who are still united with you, will cheer and praise the name of the Lord, who is revealed among them with emphasis and glory! Praise Him, all you saints, princes and powers! You holy cherubim and seraphim, one Holy! Holy! Holy! after the other; for the sake of the great penetrating love of God. Let it be known that all should be encouraged; and call up the name of the Lord to the heights, and bring glory and thanks to him. Praise to you, Oh you Eternal, most beloved Jehovah; in your holy immeasurable silence! Praise you above, for you have your evident holy throne in your heavens! Praise you, down here in the hearts of your believers with holy jubilation! Praise the Lord, my soul forever! In Jerusalem, praise the Lord! All gates and all foundations and all their precious stones, praise him. Then his brilliance will be made clear! and oh what praise! oh how triumphant! oh what a lovely sight you will see! oh you king of saints! It will be given when you have made the kingdom of our anointed head completely subject to Christ through your power: that all the powers of darkness will have been forever blocked out by your powerful hand; that death will be swallowed up in victory, and its fleeting vanity will be concluded! What praise will then ring out and be brought forth to you; when all creatures from among all fallen creatures, both men and angelic souls, and finally the chief and hereditary enemy of your name, will turn up before your footstool, and before the footstool of Jesus Christ; the eternal brought before you, they have to bow; when these spirits are raging in the darkness, and having their dominion, and yet also tormented therein, they will be seized by the wrath and fire of your justice, having been led through at their own request; that when all power is brought under the prince of the anointed king, he will hand it over to you again, together with the kingdom, and they will therefore be completely under your eternal commandment of love, together with all his firstborn, and redeemed brides of the lamb. What praise, what thanks is in your sanctuary, yea in your holiest of holies within yourself, that is offered to you and your power and wisdom! Everything, everything will melt away in your praise! The lowly dust of your soul will fall like drops in the eternal sea and will crumble; the little spark of pure spirit that you have breathed into the creatures sacred to you, will again be in you, your inextinguishable and incomprehensible fire! to come forth and glow in you forever. Then to you, the father of lights, all glory will have been offered.

Oh blessed union! How long will it be until your poor turtledove[83] will be brought before it! Therefore all praise be given to you, that can be given by your poor, weak, sinful earth surrounded by flesh and blood; offered in the deepest humility and in the most amazing silence, and deprivation itself! Now, you great God of hosts! Should it please you, speak to the babblers, that you have urged to bring forth your poor earthworms through your spirit;[84] and to all your words and promises, Amen, as your congregation takes up the assent in faith, and when the great work of restoration is complete, so soon will Amen be heard resoundingly everywhere.

Speak of the powerful sealing of your promise and our supplication, that we have performed in the name, and at the command, of our Lord and Savior Jesus.

Yes! Amen, says the true God Zebaoth: Whatever my people ask and have prayed for shall be done; so say it again, Amen! Amen!

---

83 Translator's note: "deine arme Turteltaube".

84 Translator's note: "durch deinen Geist deine arme Erd-Würmer".

𝔓reparations

FOR A PERFECT AUTHORITY OF SPIRITS[85]

♄	Aratron, is dedicated to Saturn[86]
♃	Bethor, to Jupiter
♂	Phaleg, to Mars
☉	Och, to the Sun
♀	Hagith, to Venus
☿	Ophiel, to Mercury
☽	Phuel, to the Moon

OF THE SPIRITS of the seven planets, which are also called the spirits of nature, much should be noted; but for the sake of brevity it will be passed over, and [we] shall report only the few following things about it.[87]

Their names are Aratron, Bethor, Phaleg, Och, Hagith, Ophiel, and Phuel.[88]

---

85 Translator's note: "Vorbereitende Sachen fur einen vollkommenen Geisterkenner".

86 Translator's note: "Aratron, wird Saturn zugeeignete".

87 Translator's note: "welches aber geliebter Kurtze wegen übergeben und nur folgendes weniges davon melden will".

88 Translator's note: The Olympic or Olympian spirits; from Aphorism 16 of the *Arbatel: Concerning the Magic of the Ancients* (Ibis Press, 2009, translation by Joseph Peterson, page 31): "Aratron appears on the Sabbath and the first hour of that day, and gives truthful answers about his provinces and provincials. Similarly, the others are also ordered in their days and hours. Each one of them presides for 490 years. The first cycle started sixty years before the birth of Christ, when the administration of prince Bethor began; this lasted until the year 430. He was

One of these, namely the *Spiritum Mercurii*,[89] has Albertus-Bajer, a monk of the Carmelite order,[90] of the monastery of Maria-Magdalena de Stella Nova in Italy in 1568, the 18th day of February, which was the Feast of the Glorious and Exalted Virgin Mary,[91] conjured up in the manner of an exorcist, to inquire of him about one or another of the mysteries of alchemy.

The spirit appeared and gave Albertus the following answer to the question of whether he was a good or bad spirit.

"I am neither a good nor a bad angel, but one of the seven planetary spirits who rule the middle nature; who are commanded to rule the four different parts of the world, namely the firmaments, animal, vegetable and mineral parts; and ours are seven which, through our skill, lead all earthly forces and influence of the upper world into the lower three parts, conducted through the ascending and descending parts and working therein," etc.

From knowing and dealing with these and similar types of spirits, I want to discover that secret opinion that I have drawn from the book *Sophnat Panaach*, Rabbi Abraham Ben Moses Aaron.[92]

---

followed by Phaleg up to the year 920, then Och until the year 1410, and then Hagith reigns up to 1900." Also, see page 41 of *The Secret Grimoire of Turiel*, by Marius Malchus, Weiser/Aquarian Press, 1960.

89 Translator's note: Ophiel.

90 Translator's note: See article "The Monk Albertus Bayr discovers transmutation through evoking a spirit" <https://www.alchemywebsite.com/bayr.html>.

91 Translator's note: There are numerous "Feast Days" of the Virgin Mary, and they change according to the year, although February 18th is not actually one of them. To name a few, her birth is celebrated on September 8 in the Latin Church; Mary's Assumption into heaven is celebrated on August 15 (so would possibly be celebrated on the 18th depending on the year); the Motherhood of Jesus is celebrated on January 1; Mary's Queenship is celebrated August 22.

92 Translator's note: This is probably a reference to Abraham Maimonides (also known as Rabbeinu Avraham ben ha-Rambam, and Avraham Maimuni) (1186 – December 7, 1237), who was the son of Maimonides and succeeded his father as Nagid of the Egyptian Jewish community. I could not find a record of a book by the name "Sophnat Panaach", but "Tsaphnath-Paenéach" is the name which Pharaoh gave to Joseph when he raised him to the rank of prime minister or

And he writes:

It is known that Jehovah, the Lord of all heavenly hosts, created the invisible spirits which are on high; but in such a way that they can also be on earth and with people. It is precisely these spirits that move the celestial bodies, especially the planets; because they create all the weather in the air, and give their strength to the birth of all mineral, vegetable and animal essences.

So as the soul of a person maintains the whole body with all its limbs in a firm foundation, thus the power of minerals, vegetables and animals depends on the spirits. Therefore, when one wants to inquire into the nature of spirits, one must first seek to obtain secret knowledge of such heavenly intelligences.

But here one must above all know that there are two spirits, [being] good and wicked. The good have Michael as their prince;[93] the wicked stand by the Leviathan.[94] It is the good whose customs should be sought; for they teach secrets without deception for the glory of Jehovah, and for the benefit of pure people. On the other hand, the wicked rarely come before God, wandering the whole world, and causing innumerable damage; one should abstain from them, because one has nothing but deceit to expect from them.

---

grand vizier of the kingdom (Genesis 41:45). This is an Egyptian title, and some think it means "creator", or "preserver of life". Brugsch interprets it as "governor of the district of the place of life", i.e. of Goshen, the main city which was Pithom, "the place of life". Others explain it as meaning "a revealer of secrets", or "the man to whom secrets are revealed".

93 Translator's note: Michael is an archangel, whose name means "Who is like God". See Appendix A.

94 Translator's note: The Leviathan is a kind of "sea serpent" noted in theology and mythology. It is referenced in several books of the Hebrew Bible, including Psalms, the Book of Job, the Book of Isaiah, the Book of Amos, and, according to some translations, in the Book of Jonah; it is also mentioned in the Book of Enoch. The Leviathan is often an embodiment of chaos and threatening to eat the damned in the afterlife.

And whether, like mortals, they reveal something of one or another secret, so it is only a patchwork, and against God's command, and directed to sheer deception and damage.

Who now wants to achieve the right purpose, makes a fellowship with the good spirits, so they will not only reveal themselves as often as mortals require them for the glory of God, but also reveal the most hidden things to them, and indeed take away the power of Leviathan and his spirits, so that they may keep no treasure in their possession.

But as the good spirits lead a divine life, walking before God, lowly, proper, without falsehood, holy, conducting themselves chastely and humbly; so one who wants to enter into communion with these spirits must lead a divine life, like Enoch, avoiding evil, like Job, the prince of Uz,[95] walk before God, like our fathers, Abraham and Isaac, chaste and holy, always as described in *Sophnat Panaach*.

According to this, you should know, mortal, that every spirit has its special planet through which it works; and also those stars of the zodiac, which have their nature in common with the planets; therefore, if you would now find something in the secrets of nature, so you must see which planet has its dominance over it, [and] you must make use of the same spirit that rules the planet.

Now I want to teach you first how you can participate in such revelation of the spirit. Namely, you must possess such qualities as I have told you, and seek nothing but that which can lead to glory to Jehovah and to mortal advantage.[96]

Your actions must be alone, so that you only converse with yourself in secret while alone in the mountains; but the discussion consists in desire, which is the convulsion of the mind; for you cannot talk to the spirits with your body's tongue. Therefore one has only to make conversation in the mind, with desires and human

---

95 Translator's note: "der Fürst von Uz".

96 Translator's note: "Sterblichen Ersprießlichkeit", mortal productivity.

inner requests; everything that you desire, so it will happen. For the spirit will soon unite with your thoughts, and instruct you in what you ask for. Then you want to pay attention to the alternation of your thoughts and the dreams that you become aware of in your ecstasy; because as often as the spirits want you to know how your desire may be fulfilled, they emit a tone, like [that of] an iron bell;[97] because of this, you must also have a certain little bell in your hands, so that as soon as you hear the spirit's tone, you may use your little bell to give the sign that you are ready to listen. After that, you will soon be overcome by ecstasy, in which everything will appear to you that you wished for while awake, being treasure, wisdom, health, and other goods that you demand for yourself or others; and you will also know, when you wake up, of the ways and means the spirit has taught you. However, you must do everything for the praise of Jehovah, etc.

He continues; but another spirit I know speaks in my ear not to talk any more, etc., etc.

So for now, I will keep silent about the preparation of such a magical bell, and keep its preparation in mind until the next time; but should my faithful successor also posses the arcanum,[98] then wear it at the appropriate time, in a convenient place; and write the name Adonay on the clapper,[99] and on the curve of the bell, write Tetragrammaton, and on the handle,[100] write Jesus.

Keep it pure and in a clean place, for it is an Arcanum of God;[101] you don't need any other characters and names, only the two including the third, because their virtue is inexplicable, since

---

97 Translator's note: "ehernen Schelle".

98 Translator's note: "solte aber mein getreuer Nachfolger das Arcanum auch besitzen".

99 Translator's note: "Schwengel". The bell clapper is the hanging tongue of the bell.

100 Translator's note: "Hand-Habe".

101 Translator's note: "dann es ist ein Arcanum-Gottes".

they are the greatest and highest, the two being Tetragrammaton and Adonai, with which the Hebrews and Egyptians and others created many miracles. The third name is Jesus; he is the newborn child, who is a lamb that bears the world's sin; therefor for confirmation and a divine beginning, preparation and perfection are used here. In these three are hidden all the secrets, whatever may be in heaven and in all of God's creation; therefore their virtue and wisdom may not yet be adequately spoken about in this hour, nor be found wholly, for which they are held in the highest honor, and should not be misused.

If you want to use your little bell, say:

Oh God,[102] Tetragrammaton, Adonay, I, N.,[103] your creation, ask through Jesus, wherein lies my desire in happiness, through your grace with these spirits to learn without evil, with the force of your power, Lord of hosts! Lord of all Lords, Amen.

Light to find buried treasure.[104]

R) Thurr. vel. oliban. elect.[105]

☿[106] or ♃[107]

Cerra flav[108] which is unprepared, aa.[109] and some yarn, etc.

---

102 Translator's note: "O Gott".

103 Translator's note: "I, [your name]".

104 Translator's note: Also, this candle is found in *Albertus Magnus: Being the Approved, Verified, Sympathetic and Natural Egyptian Secrets: White and Black Art For Man and Beast*, etc., De Laurence Co., 1919.

105 Original footnote: Optionally incense or fragrance. Translator's note: Olibanum is frankincense.

106 Translator's note: Sulfur.

107 Translator's note: "vel flor".

108 Translator's note: Latin for "blonde wax".

109 Original footnote: sulfur blossoms or brimstone, golden-yellow wax ["Schwefel oder Schwefelblüte, gold-gelbes Wachs"], all the same (amount).

Then make a light according to the art, and [let it] shine in every corner of the house; and where money is buried, the light goes out.

Magic glass mirror:[110]

In vulgar speech: Earth mirror[111]
which, after an original in hand, is copied with
the greatest accuracy.

Diagram 1: large talismanic diagram; hexagram in a circle with six of the sigils of the planets in the triangles of the hexagram (the sigil of the sun is excluded, but should be in the center?), and outside the hexagram are six of the talismanic sigils of the angels of the days of the week, the Solar sigil of Sunday is in the center, and also in the center is the Hebrew letters Yod Heh Vau Heh, with the basic symbol for the sun being a circle with a dot in the middle.

---

110 Translator's note: "Specul. Magic. vitr" (i.e., Speculum magicum vitreum).

111 Translator's note: "Vulg: dict: Erd-Spiegel". See *Speculum Terrae: A Magical Earth Mirror From The 17th Century*, by Frater Acher, Hadean Press, 2018.

THE HIDDEN AND TRUE PNEUMATOLOGY 25

Virgulta Divina[112]

[It] must be made of copper or brass and be a perfect triangle.

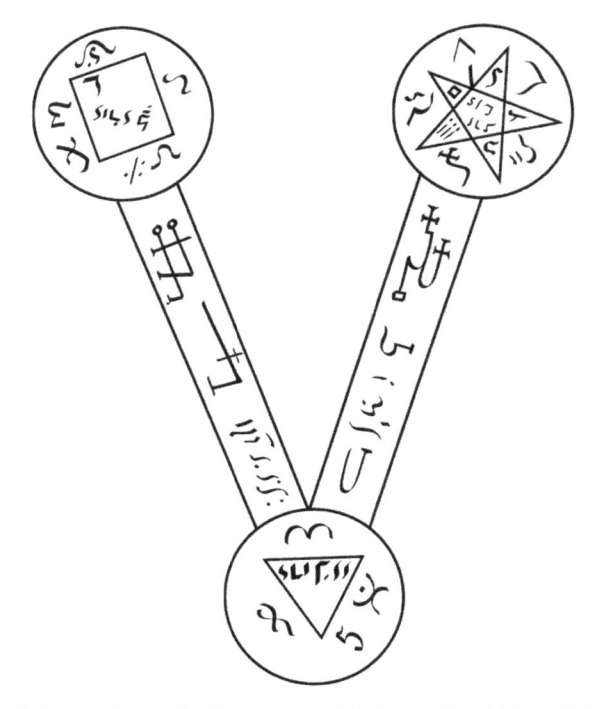

Diagram 2: large talismanic diagram; the "divine rod", which is V shaped with three circles, at each end with talismanic sigils, including symbols for lunar nodes, at the base is an inverted triangle with four symbols around it, and several inside the triangle. At the end of the left "arm" is a square with five symbols around it and several inside the square, and at the end of the right "arm" is a pentagram with five symbols around it, then symbols inside each triangle and multiple more in the center. Also, there are numerous sigils in each of the arms on the left and right side.)

---

112 Translator's note: Actually should be "Virgula Divina", meaning "divine stick (or rod)" in Latin.

The rod[113] recorded here must be made and completed in the waxing moon in the morning between nine and ten o'clock. The Hebrew letters, circles and symbols are made with cinnabar,[114] and the rod above the circle where it hangs together[115] is wrapped in the form of a third corner,[116] three times with red silk; and the subsequent invocation is also spoken three times over the rod; the first time at the beginning, the second time when it is half finished, and the third as the last time, after the rod has been completely finished.

In the name of God the Father ✠ and of God the Son ✠ and of God the Holy Spirit ✠ Amen.

I, N.N. [name] bend and conjure the metal rod,[117] through the most powerful [names] Adonai Jehovah Eloha Aph ✠, and through the most powerful [names] Adonai Jehovah Elohah Ben ✠, and through the most powerful [names] Adonai Jehovah Eloah Ruach-Hachedosch ✠ Elohim; that you have the power over everything I ask of you, to answer me through the forward stroke of your rod[118] everything that I want to know and will ask you, in and through the element of earth, that you may do this without deception.

I, N.N. [name] conjure you, rod, by the holiest [names] Adonai ✠ Zebaoth ✠ Messias ✠ Soter ✠ Emanuel ✠ Agla ✠ Tetragrammaton ✠ by the most holy creation of the world ✠ conception[119] ✠ birth ✠

---

113 Translator's note: "Ruthe", wand.

114 Translator's note: Cinnabar is the bright scarlet to brick-red form of mercury sulfide, and is the most common source ore for refining elemental mercury. It is the historic source for the brilliant red or scarlet pigment termed vermilion and associated red mercury pigments.

115 Translator's note: Or, "is attached together".

116 Translator's note: i.e., triangular.

117 Translator's note: Rüthen Metall".

118 Translator's note: "deinen vorwärts ziehenden Ruthenschlag".

119 Translator's note: "Empfängnüs".

suffering[120] ✠ and ascension[121] of Jesus Christ ✠ at the sending of the Holy Spirit ✠ by the final judgment[122] ✠.

I, N.N. [name] ask and conjure you, most holy angel and prince Ariel,[123] of the element of the earth, that you lead this rod and lead all my questions, through Adonai ✠ Agla ✠ Tetragrammaton ✠ [and] this you should assist, you holy choirs of angels, Cherubim, Seraphim, Aralim, Hasmalim, Cophnim, Throni, Potestates, Virtutes[124] et Angeli per Angelorum Angelum[125] Jesus Christ who lives and reigns in the unity of the Father ✠ and the Son ✠ and the Holy Spirit ✠ forever and ever Amen ✠ ✠ ✠.[126]

I, N.N. [name], conjure you, rod, with all the words spoken over you, Adonai, Agla, Tetragrammaton, that you answer me correctly, by the forward stroke of your rod, where is the hidden treasure, etc., etc., and I ask and conjure you, most holy angel and prince Ariel, of the element of the earth, that you lead and guide this rod, by Adonai, Agla, Tetragrammaton; this you should help, all you holy choir of angels through the angel of all angels, Jesus

---

120 Translator's note: "Leyden".

121 Translator's note: "Himmelfarth".

122 Translator's note: "bey dem Jüngsten Gericht".

123 Translator's note: An archangel, whose name means "Lion of God". See Appendix A.

124 Translator's note: Latin, "Thrones, Powers, Virtues"; orders of angels, which are different according to various texts. According to *The Hierarchie of the Blessed Angells* by Thomas Heywood (London, 1635), the orders of angels are the Seraphim, Cherubim, Thrones, Dominations, Vertues, Powers, Principats, Arch-Angells and Angells. Also, see *A Dictionary of Angels, Including the Fallen Angels* by Gustav Davidson, Free Press, 1967. Also, Cophnim likely corresponds to Ophanim, or "wheels"; Hasmalim is Hashmalim, or "living creatures", and Aralim means "warriors" or "valiant ones".

125 Translator's note: Latin, "angels by the angel of angels".

126 Translator's note: "Jesum Christum qui Vivit et regnat in unitate Patris ✠ et Filium ✠ et spiritus Sanctus ✠ in secula Seculorum Amen".

Christ, in the name of the Father ✠ and the Son ✠ and the Holy Spirit ✠ Amen.[127]

Note: As the rod is guided, it is moved with the thumb and forefinger of the right hand at the first circle, where it is connected and wrapped with silk held fast on both sides,[128] namely so that the writing is on top, etc.; so then one asks in the usual way, in the name of G. D. V. S. H. G.[129]

---

127 Translator's note: "in Nomine Patris ✠ et Fili ✠ et Spiritus Sanctus ✠ Amen".

128 Translator's note: "mit der Seide bewickelt ist auf beyden Seiten veste gehalten".

129 Translator's note: Initials for "God (GD) Father (Vater) Son (Sohn) Holy (Heilig) Ghost (Geist)". Also, see Appendix B for the prayer "Swearing Over a Divining Rod" from *Black Books of Elverum*, translation by Mary Rustad, Galde Press, 199.

The days

OF THE MONTH IN THE YEAR PREFERRED FOR THE CITATION OF THE SPIRITS

To invoke and subdue the spirits, the following days are best, in every month of the year.

Namely, take the 3rd, 4th and 8th day of the moon.

Now follow the rest of the days of the months in the year, which are preferred for the citation of the spirits.

January	3. 4. 6. 9. 11. 13.
February	2. 5. 8
March	3. 16. 17. 18.
April	12. 15.
May	7. 15. 17.
June	7. 15. 17.
July	1. 10. 19. 20.
August	5. 9. 11. 12.
September	17. 18.
December	6. 7. 11. 18.

In the following days, all evil spirits have to go to hell, and have to leave the treasures alone.
1. Holy Good Friday.[130]
2. The Friday after Easter.[131]
3. The Friday after Pentecost.
4. The Friday after Solstice.[132]
5. The Friday after [the Feast of] Simon and Judas.[133]

---

[130] Translator's note: Good Friday is a Christian holiday commemorating the crucifixion of Jesus and his death at Calvary.

[131] Translator's note: Easter Friday, or Bright Friday, is the Friday after the Christian festival of Easter. At times, this name has been confused with Good Friday, which falls a week earlier.

[132] Original footnote: Summer Solstice.

[133] Translator's note: The Apostles Simon and Jude (or Judas) are given the same feast-day because tradition holds that they were martyred together in Persia or Armenia.

𝔗𝔥𝔢 𝔱𝔯𝔲𝔢 𝔞𝔫𝔡 𝔯𝔦𝔤𝔥𝔱 𝔴𝔞𝔶

IN WHICH SPIRITS ARE CHALLENGED AND SPOKEN TO

HERE FOLLOWS THE true and right way in which spirits are to be challenged and spoken to, etc., etc.

Never without Michael's strength.

THE MAIN RULES[134]
which an exorcist has to observe are as follows.

I.
Whenever you want to do something with the spirits, whether they are good or bad, pray diligently to God and live godly, otherwise you will raise little or nothing at all.

II.
Before you undertake anything of the sort, take Holy Communion and banish all hostility towards your neighbor from your heart.

III.
You should also protect yourself with sacred things, which one tends to hang on to and wear on the body, namely *sigilla* or pieces of attachment that are sanctified with baptismal water and no less; that you write the Most Holy Name כשרע[135] with chalk on the walls and all the corners of your bedchamber, for when the spirits or devils[136] notice your advances, they will put obstacles and stones in

---

134 Translator's note: "Haubt Reguln"; i.e., "haupt Regeln".

135 Original footnote: Hebrew: Protection. Translator's note: Kaph Shin Resh Ayin.

136 Translator's note: "denn wann die Geister oder Teufel".

your way, and many pitfalls, so that you may not bring anything to stand against them.

IV.

If you are married, then abstain for nine days from intercourse, and all lewd indecent thoughts and meddlesome things; and keep yourself chaste and pure as much as humanly possible.

V.

During these nine days you should also diligently distribute alms[137], and employ other works of mercy to the poor and needy people.

VI.

You must also live soberly and moderately as much as possible during this time; and beware of eating and drinking more than is necessary to sustain the body, for nature is content with little.[138]

VII.

During this time you should not curse or swear, or speak useless things against God's name. You should also not have the wicked enemy's name in your mouth; otherwise you will commit a serious sin, and make yourself unfit for your plan.

VIII.

Just put a firm trust in God the Almighty and his son Jesus, and you will do wondrous things, yea conquer the devil himself; but if you lack the aforesaid trust, you would thresh empty straw[139] in everything; indeed the spirits would only laugh at you when they notice such a one, and you would furthermore have to learn to

---

137 Translator's note: "Allmosen". Almsgiving is the practice of giving money or food to poor people.

138 Translator's note: "den die Natur ist mit Wenigen vergnüget".

139 Translator's note: "leeres Stroh dreschen".

THE HIDDEN AND TRUE PNEUMATOLOGY 33

your loss[140] what you had started.

Your shirt, which you must have inherited from your ancestors, should be clean and washed; and the exorcist must wear this over his clothes. Both the evil and the good spirits love cleanliness; the latter because they are without the pure spirits; the former, however, because they were also transfigured in uncleanness, and then also have bodies transfigured in their damnation, and the same can be driven out and irritated[141] with nothing more than stinking and unclean things.

But with that, dear reader, here all long-windedness flees,[142] and you may carry only the core of the incantations and what belongs to them. Just note the following, which is indispensable for this possession; namely that all times, all days, and all hours, indeed all minutes, are of the Lord, and standing by his hand and power. There are certain days and nights which have been found better, more dignified and more formidable for summoning those evil spirits, since they are whole. On Christmas night, the Good Friday on which Christ died, the night before salvation. Easter day comes, the day of Pentecost, and Ascension night, as well as the day of the archangel Michael,[143] which is very deadly to the evil spirits; so one has the experience that on such days and nights they are far more sad, more gentle and [they will] testify to one more obediently. One can then conclude the intention of the incantation easily; one also likes to take Saturdays as well, since this planet, just as the people born in this planetary hour, not only poses a danger to the evil spirits, but is rather contrary to their nature, so that they flee [from] this planet as well as such people far more than others; therefore if the exorcist is born under the rulership of Saturn, the

---

140 Translator's note: "Mit Schaden erfahren".

141 Translator's note: "in Harnisch gebracht" (literally "brought into armor", but idiomatically meaning "up in arms", etc.).

142 Translator's note: "alle Weitläuffigkeit fliehen".

143 Translator's note: September 29th is the Feast of Saint Michael the Archangel.

spirits will never appear to him; if he immediately invokes them, they will flee anyway.

Noon or midnight is the most convenient and best time for the incantations. The exorcist must also take care that the sky is always clear or starry, because in cloudy and unfriendly weather it is dangerous to take in hand, the spirits living in the air then being as nasty, wild and insidious as the weather.

It is also necessary for the exorcist to know the signs of their planets, which will come forth several times in the formation of circles and incantations; when one wishes to make a righteous summoning, one has but to write the signs in the following manner.

The sign of Saturn, which is otherwise written among the planets in general as (symbol for Saturn), when invoking is so constituted in a more holy and more secret way.

Sigil of Saturn   Intelligence of Saturn

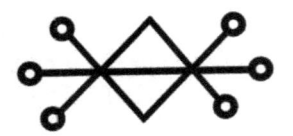

Demon of Saturn

THE HIDDEN AND TRUE PNEUMATOLOGY

Sigil of Jupiter

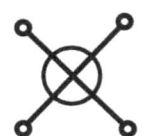

Intelligence of Jupiter

Demon of Jupiter

Sigil of Mars

Intelligence of Mars

Demon of Mars

36 PNEUMATOLOGIA OCCULTA ET VERA

Sigil of the Sun

Intelligence of the Sun

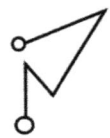

Demon of the Sun

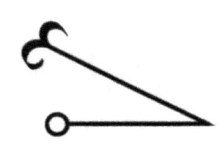

Sigil of Venus

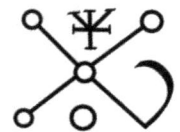

Intelligence of Venus

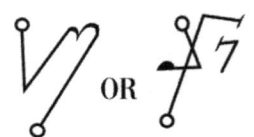

OR

Demon of Venus

THE HIDDEN AND TRUE PNEUMATOLOGY

Sigil of Mercury

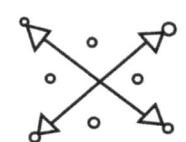

Intelligence of Mercury

Demon of Mercury

Sigil of the Moon

Intelligence of the Moon

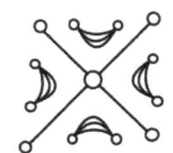

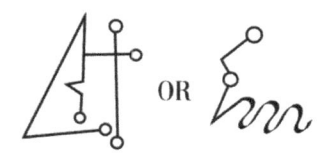

OR

Demon of the Moon

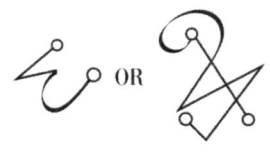

OR

The angels and devils

DEAR READER, don't be surprised that I write the same as Cornelius Agrippa, who also reports this; it was only done so that you should know that other signs besides these are wrong. While I have shown you here by the shortest route in the clearest possible way how one can invoke, dig and raise treasures buried under or in the earth, it was indisputably necessary to add these and other signs, so that this little work is not just a compendium, but also perfect, as you will indeed find it to be.[144]

Furthermore, one has to be careful, just as there are in heaven and heavenly joys certain degrees, different rewards, all sorts of offices and duties, in the same way [that] there are different kinds of bliss, so it is also among those who are damned, for the

---

[144] Translator's note: In *Three Books of Occult Philosophy*, edited by Donald Tyson, Llewelyn, 1993/2019, see chapter xxii, pages 319–327. The sigils presented here are somewhat similar to those given in Agrippa, with some differences. But also, see pages 747–751, where the editor makes note of these sigils by use of "Magic Squares" (Appendix V). The diagrams reproduced there have some similarities but are mostly quite different, except the seals of the planets do match up generally, which are on pages 743–745. Agrippa notes that Saturn's Intelligence is Agiel, its Spirit Zazel. Jupiter's Intelligence is Johphiel, its Spirit Hismael. Mars's Intelligence is Graphiel, its Spirit Barzabel. The Sun's Intelligence is Nachiel, its Spirit Sorath. Venus's Intelligence is Hagiel, its Spirit Kedemel, and its Intelligences the Bne Seraphim. Mercury's Intelligence is Tiriel, its Spirit Taphthartharath. The Moon's Intelligence is not specified, its Spirit is Hasmodai, Spirit of Spirits is Schedbarschemoth Schartathan, and Intelligence of the Intelligences is Malcha betharsithim hed beruah schehakim. Also, see the new edition translated by Eric Purdue, Inner Traditions, 2021, pages 338–348, where the sigils are mostly similar with just a few being somewhat different. Also, *The Secret Grimoire of Turiel*, by Marius Malchus, Weiser/Aquarian Press, 1960, pages 32–35, where there is a more detailed list of various planetary spirits, intelligences, and messengers.

torments and places are also differentiated there, so that one level is always larger or smaller; on the other hand, in heaven there are nine generations of the archangels,[145] being Seraphim, Cherubim, Thrones, Rulers, Powers, Virtuosities, Principalities,[146] archangels, and angels.

There are also nine angels established in heaven, namely Metatron, Orphaniel, Zaphiel, Camael, Raphael, Haniel, Michael, and Gabriel.[147]

Eight are the rewards of souls, being the heritage,[148] incorporation, power, victory, and vision of God, the kingdom and everlasting joy.

Twelve are the angels assigned to the heavenly signs, being Machidiel, Aomodel, Ambriel, Verchiel, Hamabiel, Zuriel, Barbiel, Annachiel, Hannael, Gabriel, and Barchiel.[149]

---

145 Translator's note: "Ertz Engel".

146 Translator's note: "Herrschaften, Mächte, Tugendwürkende, Fürstenthümer".

147 Translator's note: "es sind auch neun Engel dem Himmel furgesetzet, namentlich Metanon [sic], Orphaniel, Zaphiel, Camäel, Raphäel, Haniel, Michael, und Gabriel". There are only eight angels listed here, but the archangel Uriel is likely the missing name. Each angel has a lengthy description of their attributes; for example, Metatron is the first (and last) of the 10 archangels of the Briatic world, also known as the "King of Angels", and prince of the divine face or presence, chancellor of heaven, angel of the covenant, chief of the ministering angels. He is charged with the sustenance of mankind (see *A Dictionary of Angels* by Gustav Davidson, Free Press, 1967.

148 Translator's note: "Erbschaft", legacy.

149 Translator's note: "zwolf Engel die denen himmlischen Zeichen fürgesetzet werden, als Machidiel, Aomodel, Ambriel, Verchiel, Hamabiel, Zuriel, Barbiel, Annachiel, Hannael, Gabriel, und Barchiel". There are only eleven angels listed here. Each is known for various reasons, these are taken from *The Magus, or Celestial Intelligencer* by Francis Barrett (which draws heavily on Agrippa's *Three Books of Occult Philosophy*): Machidiel, ruler of the zodiac sign Aries, and governing angel of the month of March; Aomodel, or Asmodel, ruler of the sign Taurus; Ambriel, ruler over Gemini; Verchuel, or Verchiel, ruler over Leo; Hamabiel, or Hamaliel, ruler over Virgo; Zuriel, ruler over Libra; Barbiel, or Barchiel, ruler over Scorpio; Annachiel, or Advachiel or Adnachiel, ruler over Sagittarius; Hannael, or Hamael, ruler over Capricorn; Gabriel (actually should be Cambiel),

Now follow the orders of damned and hellish spirits[150] and their degrees, which are the following.

The devils, however, are divided into nine classes or orders, and in fact, subsequent measures.

First of all among false gods, those who presume to take the name of God for themselves, and who as gods want to be worshiped with sacrifice and adoration, like that devil who said to the Son of God: "I will give you all of this if you fall down and worship me", and the most venerable prince among them was Beelzebub.[151]

In the next class belong the lying spirits,[152] who rose up as a lying spirit from the mouth of the prophet Ahab,[153] among whom the foremost is the serpent Python, from which the pagan Apollo[154] was called the Pythian, and the Pythonic Woman by Samuel;[155] this kind of devil has formerly interfered with the oracles,[156] namely where one asked the idols for advice.

Third, the vessels of impurity[157] which cause all evil and teach evil arts; such is the one who, under the name of Theutus in Plato,

---

ruler over Aquarius; Barchiel, ruler over Pisces. Missing from this text is Muriel, ruler over the sign Cancer. Also, see Appendix A.

150 Translator's note: "verdammten und höllischen Geistern Ordnungen".

151 Translator's note: Beelzebub or Beelzebul is a name derived from the title of a Philistine god, formerly worshiped in Ekron, and later adopted by some Abrahamic religions as a major demon. The name Beelzebub is associated with the Canaanite god Baal, and in Christian theology, another name for Satan. It is also a demon prince in *The Book of Abramelin*.

152 Translator's note: "in die andere Classe gehören die Lügen-Geister".

153 Translator's note: Ahab was the seventh king of Israel, the son and successor of King Omri and the husband of Jezebel of Sidon, according to the Hebrew Bible (1 Kings 16:29–34). Ahab is described as being a wicked king, particularly for condoning Jezebel's influence on religious policies.

154 Translator's note: "der heydnische Apollo".

155 Translator's note: See Appendix A.

156 Translator's note: "diese Arth der Teufel hat sich ehehin unter denen Oraculis... mit eingemischet".

157 Translator's note: "die Gefäße der Unreinigkeit".

invented the strange way of playing the board game.[158] This is the one of which Jacob spoke in the first book of Moses in the blessing upon Simeon and Levi. 49:5–6: "in their dwellings are vessels of impurity; their swords are murderous weapons; my soul come not into their counsel."[159] The foremost is Belial.[160]

Fourth, the spirits of vengeance, whose chief is Asmod, or Asmodeus in Tobia.[161]

Fifth, the magical spirits who imitate miracles and serve witches and fiends, but seduce the people like the serpent did Eve,[162] whose chief is called Sathan.[163]

Sixth, those who have their activity in the air and mingle with thunder, lightning and hail, which infect the air and arouse the pestilence, and cause other misfortunes; these devils are indicated in John's revelation by the four angels,[164] to whom power is given

---

158 Translator's note: "Brett-Spiel". The word "Brett" literally means board, and "Spiel" means game. The only "board game" that I can think of here is the Ouija board, or otherwise the tarot, which is not technically a "board game".

159 Translator's note: In Genesis 49:5–49:6 from the King James version: "Simeon and Levi are brethren; instruments of cruelty are in their habitations. O my soul, come not thou into their secret; unto their assembly, mine honour, be not thou united: for in their anger they slew a man, and in their self will they digged down a wall."

160 Translator's note: Belial is the 68th spirit of the Goetia, considered a "demon king". In Hebrew, *belial* is a word "used to characterize the wicked or worthless". There are many references to Belial in various texts, including a classic German work entitled *Das Buch Belial*, by Jacobus de Teramo, published in Augsberg, 1473.

161 Translator's note: "Tobias" or "Tobit"; a reference to the Book of Tobit. Asmodeus is the 32nd spirit of the Goetia, considered a "demon king". In Judeo-Islamic lore, he is the king of the earthly spirits, mostly known from the deuterocanonical Book of Tobit, in which he is the primary antagonist. Also, a demon prince in *The Book of Abramelin*. There are also numerous references to Asmodeus in various other texts. See Appendix A.

162 Translator's note: "wie die Schlange Evam"; a reference to the serpent who "tempted" Eve in the Garden.

163 Translator's note: Or "Satan". The prince of evil and adversary of God. Many volumes have been written about Satan. See Appendix A.

164 Translator's note: The Book of Revelation, or Apocalypse of John.

to harm the earth and the sea; the foremost of whom is called Meierim,[165] namely the midday devil,[166] of whom Paul testifies to the Ephesians that he has his work in the children of unbelief.

The seventh order or place is of the Furies, which cause all evil, such as discord, war and devastation; their superior according to the Greek language in the Revelation of John is Apollio,[167] but Abaddon in Hebrew, which means in German a corruptor.[168][169]

In the eighth order are the vices and watchers, whose principal is Astharoth, that is the watcher who searches out people; and in the Greek he is called Diabolus, who accuses our brothers day and night for God.[170]

The last order is the tempting devils,[171] and those who pursue people, who look after each and every human being and sit on their caps.[172] They are actually called the evil spirits, and their

---

165 Translator's note: Or "Meririm". Also related to the name Satan, identified as the evil power whom Paul in Ephesians called "prince of the power of the air". See Appendix A.

166 Translator's note: "der Mittags-Teufel".

167 Translator's note: "deren Oberster nach der Grichischen Sprache in der Offenbahrung Joannis Apollio".

168 Translator's note: "Verderber ".

169 Translator's note: In the Book of Revelation of the New Testament, an angel called Abaddon is described as the king of an army of locusts; his name is first transcribed in Koine Greek (Revelation 9:11—"whose name in Hebrew is Abaddon") as Ἀβαδδών, and then translated Ἀπολλύων, Apollyon. Also, in the Qliphoth, Abaddon is the "fourth hell", ruled over by Astaroth. See *Goetic Evocation* by Steve Savedow, Hadean Press, 2022.

170 Translator's note: Astaroth is the 29th spirit of the Goetia, and the Great Duke of Hell in the first hierarchy with Beelzebub and Lucifer; he is part of the evil trinity. He is a male figure most likely named after the Near Eastern goddess Astarte. Diabolus is a name of Astaroth, and he was aided in the war against Shaddai (God) by Apollyon, Python, Cerberus, Legion, Lucifer, and other "diabolonians" (*The Holy War*, John Bunyan). See *A Dictionary of Angels* by Gustav Davidson.

171 Translator's note: "der Versuch Teufel".

172 Translator's note: "und auf der Hauben seynd".

chief is Mamon, or the Desire.[173]

There are six among them, who in hell are called the devils originating and inciting all harm, namely Aetus, Megalosius, Ormenus, Lycus, Kyeon, and Minos.[174]

There are also seven dwellings in hell, in which dwell the subterranean spirits and devils, described by Rabbi Joseph of Castile[175] as follows: hell, the gate of death, the shadow of death, the port of doom, the death of rabble, perdition, and the abyss.

There are also eight kinds of torments of the damned, namely:[176]

---

173 Translator's note: "Mamon, oder die Begierde". Mammon in the New Testament of the Bible is commonly thought to signify money, material wealth, or any entity that promises wealth, and is associated with the greedy pursuit of gain. In the Middle Ages it was often personified and sometimes included among the seven princes of hell. In Davidson's *Dictionary of Angels*, Mammon is described as a fallen angel now ruling in hell, and in the *Dictionnaire Infernal* by Colin de Plancy, is certified as "Hell's ambassador to England". Also, this figure may be identified with Amaimon, who is a demon prince in *The Book of Abramelin*.

174 Translator's note: These names are of the Telchines, which in Greek mythology are a sort of "demi-god", and the original inhabitants of the island of Rhodes. They were also known in Crete and Cyprus. Their parents were said to be either Pontus and Gaia, or Tartarus and Nemesis. Depending on the source, their names include Damon (Demonax), Mylas, Atabyrius, Antaeus, Actaeus, Megalesius, Ormenos, Lycus, Nicon and Mimon, Chryson, Argyron and Chalcon. Also, some female Telchines were named Makelo, Dexithea, Halia, and Lysagora. See Appendix A.

175 Translator's note: "Joseph Rabbi Castiliensis", i.e. Joseph ben Abraham Gikatilla.

176 Translator's note: In relation to the hells of the Qliphoth, see *Goetic Evocation* by Savedow, chapter 4 on the Qliphoth and Appendix C being "The Qliphoth of the Golden Dawn". This was originally an instructional paper for initiates of the Isis-Urania temple of the Golden Dawn, transcribed circa 1900, and later re-published in "The Roots of the Golden Dawn" series by R.A. Gilbert, as *The Sorcerer and His Apprentice*, Aquarian Press, 1983.

There are various descriptions of the different levels of hell, most notably in John Milton's *Paradise Lost* (London, 1667). In Dante Alighieri's epic poem *Inferno* (the first portion of *Divine Comedy*, c. 1320) the nine circles of hell are, from top to bottom, Limbo, Lust, Gluttony, Greed, Anger, Heresy, Violence, Fraud

The prison[177]
The pit where there is no water[178]
The eternal death[179]
The court[180]
God's wrath[181]
Cast out from before God's face[182]
Torment in hell[183]
Fear in hell[184]

Saturn alone stands against these devils, especially when digging up hidden treasures, in that Saturn is placed over the earth,[185] which is an element of Saturn. Hence it is the sign of Saturn in the exorcist's circle, [that] gives him assurance the spirits not only cannot harm him, but rather will flee as soon as they see anything Saturnian in the circle.

So the devils also have certain levels and positions among themselves, as already mentioned; namely, there are chiefs, servants, slaves,[186] subservient spirits, miners and the like; one of

---

and Treachery (obviously many based on the "seven deadly sins"). Also, in *Three Books of Occult Philosophy* by Agrippa (ed. Donald Tyson, Llewelyn, 1993/2019), chapter 10 of book II, the seven levels of hell are noted as Gihenam or hell, gates of death, shadow of death, pit of destruction, clay of death (miry clay), perdition (or destruction), and depth of the earth (or grave).

177 Translator's note: "Gefängniß".

178 Translator's note: "Grube da kein Wasser inne ist."

179 Translator's note: "Ewige Todt".

180 Translator's note: "Gericht".

181 Translator's note: "Zorn Gottes".

182 Translator's note: "Verstoßung von Gottes Angesicht".

183 Translator's note: "Höllen Quaal".

184 Translator's note: "Höllen Angst".

185 Translator's note: Saturnus is also the Roman God of agriculture and farming.

186 Translator's note: "Oberhaubter, Bediente, Diener".

whom has to command the other, and the latter has to obey.

But it was necessary here to mention their degrees and order, so that the exorcist would know how to make a distinction between them; so that he would not invoke the wrong spirits, and perhaps expect something that was not his due; but meet everyone according to his status, office and duties; because when they are invoked, they diligently notice whether you are doing it right, and if you only miss a single word, that is what happens to your body.[187]

So you should think about it and consider who you are dealing with, being evil spirits, namely fallen spirits, which were angels in the beginning, usually appearing in the following form.

Just as the holy angels and heavenly spirits mostly appear in human form, and indeed as beautiful young men, so the devils and evil spirits, on the other hand, can usually be seen in abominable forms; but it is not a question here of the matter of the form, which I let be in its place, but of the form or shape itself, touching here only on what the exorcist needs to know.

And indeed they sometimes appear in the shape of a roaring lion, or also of a bear, elephant, monkey, dog, dragon, or whatever other beautiful[188] figures there are.

But the guardians of their treasure also belong to this level and order, which can generally be seen as black or fiery dogs, toads or night owls;[189] and [they] give the exorcist much trouble until he gets hold of them, and then snatches the treasure from them. There is no buried treasure that does not have its guardian, yet there are often two or three, depending on the value or quantity of the same; but the poor souls [who] wander about in the dark and frighten people, they are either black or white, it is all the same, and therefore nothing special, because while they may be black or white, they are still damned, and in the devil's power until the

---

187 Translator's note: "so ist es um deinen Leib geschehen".

188 Translator's note: "schöne".

189 Translator's note: "Krotten oder Nacht Eulen".

judgment of God,[190] or from the time determined by God; who gives them his hands or touches them, they burn him; even though they sometimes cry and pretend they want to be saved, they are not to be trusted, harming people where they can. So you should be careful and carry out your incantation with sound reason and clearly, if you want to release such a wandering soul and bring it to rest.

There are also three different rulerships of these blessed spirits, each of which consists of five different spirits, namely:[191]

1. Seraphim.	2. Cherubim.	3. Thrones.
1. Rulers.	2. Powers.	3. Forces.
1. Principalities.	2. Archangels.	3. Angels.
1. Innocents.	2. Martyrs.	3. Confessors.
1. Patriarchs.	2. Prophets.	3. Apostles.

Four angels as superiors at the four ends of heaven:[192]
1. Michael. 2. Raphael. 3. Gabriel. 4. Uriel.
and these are also called the four Archangels.

They are over these too, four set over the four elements, specifically so:

| שרף | חרוב | תרשש | אריאל |
| Seraph. | Cherub. | Tharsis. | Ariel. |

---

190 Translator's note: derer Teufel Gewalt biß zu dem Gerichte Gottes".

191 Translator's note: The orders of the hierarchy of angels, see *The Hierarchie of the Blessed Angells* by Thomas Heywood, and *A Dictionary of Angels* by Gustav Davidson.

192 Translator's note: The four archangels each have lengthy descriptions and are well known in Hebrew mythology, qabalistic lore and occultism. See Appendix A.

Four elements together with their signs and meanings:

Earth	Water	Air	Fire
ꙮ	ꙫ	missing in manuscript	ꙩ

Four parts of the world: the east, west, north and south.[193]

Four princes of devils which in the four elements can do harm: Samael, Alzazel, Azael, Machazael.[194]

Four rivers of hell: Phlegeton, Cocythis, Stix, Acheron.[195]

Four of the most noble princes of hell: Lucifer, Leviathan, Sathan, Belial.[196]

Eight other princes, whom the previous four have to command or which are under them:

Astharoth, Magoth, Asmodi, Beelzebub.

Oriens, Paymon, Ariton, Amaymon.[197]

Four chief devils, that rule the four parts of the air:

Oriens, Paymon, Egyn or Ariton, Amaymon.

---

193 Translator's note: "der Aufgang, Niedergang, Mitternacht und Mittag" (literally "rising, falling, midnight and noon").

194 Translator's note: Samael is sometimes identified as Satan, and is also an archangel in Talmudic and post-Talmudic lore; a figure who is the accuser (Ha-Satan), seducer, and destroyer (Mashhit). Alzazel or Azazel has several origin myths, as in the Book of Enoch where he is one of the chiefs of the 200 fallen angels, and "taught men to fashion swords and shields", etc. Azael or Azrael is the angel of death in some Abrahamic religions, namely Islam and some traditions of Judaism. Machazael or Machasiel is an angel invoked from the south (see the *Heptameron*) and is listed among the intelligences of the Sun (see *The Secret Grimoire of Turiel*). See *A Dictionary of Angels* by Gustav Davidson.

195 Translator's note: There are actually five rivers encircling Hades in Greek mythology: the Styx, Phlegethon, Lethe, Acheron and Cocytus.

196 Translator's note: The four kings from *The Book of Abramelin*. See *The Book of Abramelin*, compiled and edited by Georg Dehn, translated by Steven Guth, Ibis Press, 2006, page 23, 39, 156.

197 Translator's note: These are the eight demon princes (or dukes) of *The Book of Abramelin*. See ibid., pages 156–160, 170–171, and 283–297.

The good angels

WHO RULE EVERY DAY OF THE WEEK

Now following are the good angels, who rule every day of the week, with their signs.[198]

The angel of Sunday is Michael, his sign is:

The planet of this day is ☉ and of the sign ♌.
The angels associated are named Dardiel and Hurtapel.
The angel of the air[199] on this day is called Varcan the king.
And the wind Boreas the north wind.
The smoke that goes with it consists of red sandalwood.[200]

The name of the angel of Monday is Gabriel, his sign is:

The planet of this day is ☽ and of the sign ♐.
The angels associated are named Michael and Samael.
The name of the angel of the air on this day is Arcan the king, and the name of the wind is Zephyrus,

---

198 Translator's note: The angels and talismans here match those in the Heptameron.

199 Translator's note: "Engel der Lufft".

200 Translator's note: See *The Fourth Book of Occult Philosophy*, editor Stephen Skinner, Ibis Press, 2005, pages 76–77. Also *The Heptameron or Magical Elements of Peter de Abano*, Ouroboros Press, 2003.

the wind blowing from the west.[201]
The smoke consists of aloe.[202]

Tuesday's angel is Samael, his sign is:

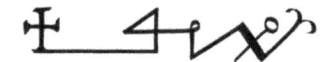

The planet of the day is ♂ and the sign is ♈ ♏.
The angels associated with it are called Satael and Amaliel.
The angel of the air is called Samex the king of the winds, but Subsolanus, who blows from the very place where the Sun rises, when it makes day and night equal.
The smoke is made of pepper.[203]

The angel of Wednesday is Raphael, but his sign:

The planet of this day is ☿ and its sign also ♐ ♏.
The angels associated to him are named Miel and Saraphiel.
The angel of the air is called Medial, or Modial, the king.
But the wind is called Africus, the south-west wind.
The smoke consists of mastics.[204]

---

201 Translator's note: "der von Niedergang wehende Wind".

202 Translator's note: *The Fourth Book of Occult Philosophy*, editor Stephen Skinner, Ibis Press, 2005, pages 78–79.

203 Translator's note: Ibid., pages 80–82.

204 Translator's note: Mastic is a resin obtained from the mastic tree (Pistacia) and, like other natural resins, is produced in "tears" or droplets. See also *The Fourth Book of Occult Philosophy*, editor Stephen Skinner, Ibis Press, 2005, pages 83–85.

The angel of Thursdays is Sachiel, but his sign:

The planet of this day is ♃ and of the sign ♓ or ♓.
The angels associated with it are called Castael and Asasiel.
The angel of the air is called Suth the king.
But the wind is called Auster the south wind.
The smoke consists of saffron.[205]

The angel of Friday is Anael, his sign is:

The planet of this day is ♀ and the sign ♉ ♎.
The angels associated to it are called Rachiel and Sachiel.
The angel of the air is called Sarabotref the king.
But the wind is Zephyrus the west wind.
The smoke is Costus.[206][207]

Saturday's angel is Cassiel, his sign is:

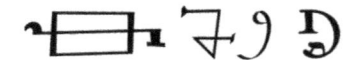

The planet of this day is ♄ and of the sign ♒.
The angels associated with it are called Machatan and Uriel.

---

[205] Translator's note: Ibid., pages 85–87.

[206] Translator's note: Costus is a group of herbaceous perennial plants in the family *Costaceae*, described by Linnaeus as a genus in 1753. It was formerly known as *Hellenia* after the Finnish botanist Carl Niclas von Hellens. It is widespread through tropical and subtropical regions of Asia, Africa, and the Americas.

[207] Translator's note: *The Fourth Book of Occult Philosophy*, editor Stephen Skinner, Ibis Press, 2005, pages 88–89.

The angel of the air is called Maymon the king.
But the wind is Afrus the south-west wind.
The smoke consists of sulphur.[208]

Among these days, Sunday and Monday along with Friday are the best; on the first day you will get gold, but on the other two silver.

Before we proceed to the formation of the circle and the incantations themselves, it is still necessary to remember that one should beware of the serving spirits, which one calls *Spiritus Familiares*[209]. These are, so to speak, the brat fools[210] among the devils, loose and mocking thieves, who play no more than tricks; so that they only deceive people and the conjurer or exorcist, and make them err in their plan, at which they then laugh up their sleeves when it suits them.

So when you have a treasure buried somewhere and it is ready to be raised, so that everything that is necessary has already been done, and it is now up to you to get what you wish and desire at all times; then they will incite every imaginable fear and terror in you, through which they will force you to speak, or try to blow in a goat's horn,[211] or that you should even run away and abandon everything.

But if they manage to do something like this, they immediately disappear laughing loudly.

So that the exorcist may beware of their pranks, it is very useful and advisable, and also highly necessary, that he should have an exact knowledge of their nature, positions, shapes, appearances and indications; no less how they should be expelled

---

208 Translator's note: Ibid., pages 91–92.
209 Translator's note: Familiar spirits.
210 Translator's note: "Fratz-Narren".
211 Translator's note: "Bocks-Horn".

and conjured,[212] so that they cannot be a hindrance to him.

But it remains to control the spirits, and in his power Aratron, who is placed over them; who if he wants, can also give serving spirits, or *Spiritus Familiares*. He can also transform the treasures into coals, and in turn the coals into treasures; in the same way not only make everything invisible, but turn it into stone in an instant.

Therefore, it is to be known that ministering spirits are reported to sometimes appear in the form of a dragon, bear, toad, raven or even a camel, even as people who are torn to pieces.

Now, if these are Saturnian spirits, then they create a storm wind, with a kind of earthquake; but if they are Jovial, they awaken and make sheets of rain with thunder and lightning.

Others, however, effect something else in their own way; whoever does not know the nature of the spirits cannot get along with them either, or bring about a powerful incantation. So be careful that they don't laugh at you or thwart your plans; because this is their intention when they appear. They often come like a strong wind, but so you should and can deal with them, I want you, dear reader, to say the following, for it is extremely necessary so that you don't lose your life and your soul at the same time; I beg you, for God's sake, believe me, that in this small and secret little work, I won't give you a word in vain. I indeed would have had very many who would have paid me dearly enough for these lessons, if I wasn't worried [that] they might abuse the science.

Here then lies the secret of all secrets. I have accomplished much by God's help in this way, which I use myself. I have laughed at others who boasted that they knew how to dig for treasure.

A righteous exorcist who believes in Jesus Christ diligently invokes him, and does this work through his holy name. He can also force the very highest prince of the devils to give you everything, without harming a hair of your head; because it is certainly, as

---

212 Translator's note: In traditional grimoire texts, the spirit is given "the license to depart" and is bound by the operator.

our beloved savior Jesus said, "if you have faith, say this to the mountains: Rise up from there, yes; by believing in me you can raise the dead, and do all the works that I do, if only you believe in me, and in he who sent me; in the name of Jehovah, the maker of heaven and earth; for He is the Lord of the heavenly host Sabaoth. Why shouldn't he also be able to drive the devils away?"

But we want to continue on further, and to come a little closer to the most secret work itself.

For assistance we call on the Most Holy Trinity,
God the Father ✠
God the Son ✠ and
God the Holy Spirit ✠.

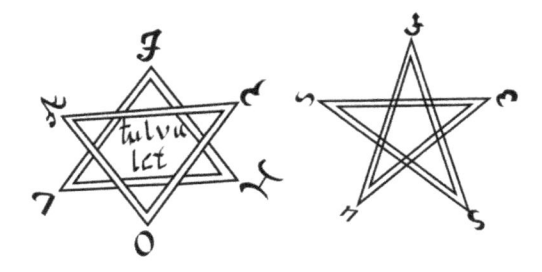

The triune God JEHOVA rules.[213]

---

213 Translator's note: "Das walte der dreyeinige Gott JEHOVA". The core belief there is One God, who is Father, Son, and Holy Spirit; that God is three persons—the Father, the Son who is Jesus, and the Holy Spirit which is the spirit of God's grace. Other ways of referring to the Trinity are "the Threefold God" and "the Three-in-One", three persons in one God.

Dear Reader,

In the name of Jesus, who is the seed of woman, and who crushes the serpent's head, I now open to you the secret of treasure, so that it may open to you the underground treasures buried by miserly and evil souls; but I beg you again, for God's sake beware of security, and remember everything that is written here, so that you understand everything well, and do not miss the right path by misusing it.

If you notice a buried treasure in a place nearby, or let yourself see a spirit or the soul that buried it, then go to the same place early in the morning twilight before sunrise, and sober; and you should have no one but God with you. Say your morning prayers, and mark yourself with the sign of the Holy Cross on your forehead, mouth, and breast; then whether it be in a room or cellar, under the open sky or under a roof, you must have four small pieces of paper with you, whereupon the holy name of Jesus is written, and thereunder these words:

In the name of Jesus, every knee must bow, which is in heaven, on earth, and under the earth; flee, therefore, you unclean spirits, for here is Jesus.

You must bury these four little pieces of paper in four corners, so that you make a square with them. When this happens, fall down on your knees and say the following little prayer with a fervently devoted heart.

Lord God, creator of heaven and earth. You are ruler of the angels; also of all other good and evil spirits; before whose mighty voice, the damned will tremble. Behold, I am a man created in your image, though I am [made of] earth and ashes; but through your only son, born of the Virgin Mary, who is the one true woman-seed of Jesus; who redeems my sinful soul from the power of the devil and from eternal death; so I ask of you, Merciful God! you who are Lord and King of the Heavenly Host, grant mercy that this poor soul, wandering around in the darkness, may be redeemed, and may rest until the Judgment, so it does not continue to frighten people; and this be granted to me which I ask of you, in the name of your son, Jesus Christ, who is with you, together with the Holy Spirit. Be there praise, honor and glory, forever and ever.

Little sigh.[214]

Lord I believe; help my weakness in belief through Jesus Christ, Amen.

The spirit or the phantom[215] becomes so loud under this prayer, that you will be able to hear it crying, or at least sighing audibly; although you see nothing right away, it will be close to you; and indeed it is for this reason that [the spirit] shall be gladly set free; but when the guardians of the treasure notice it, [they] will cause all sorts of annoyance and plague to the poor soul; [they] will make a fuss that you should be afraid, but only be of good courage and trust in God; for they are not only already hindered, and as it were, bound so that they cannot harm you, but also because of the little papers buried in the four corners or nooks of this place, they will no longer be able, according to their evil habit, to cause the treasure to decay, or move it somewhere else.

Now when this happens, get up again and mark yourself again with the sign of the Holy Cross, and speak in the name of God the Father ✠ God the Son ✠ and God the Holy Spirit ✠.

When you have done this, you must neither wait nor absent yourself any longer than three days to make the incantation; meanwhile the spirit will sigh and also cry loudly, so that everyone will be able to hear. He will be extremely restless, until the hour of his release from haunting is at hand. The guardians of the treasure will not only torment him, but also threaten him in every

---

214 Translator's note: "Seuffzerlein".

215 Translator's note: "der Geist oder das Gespinnst".

conceivable way, if he willingly consented to the incantation.

During these three days, the exorcist must purchase four wax lights over which a Holy Mass is read, and which are also consecrated at the same time, because if this did not happen, the hellish guardians of the treasure would extinguish the lights, thereby putting you in great danger to both body and soul.

It is also necessary that the exorcist make a special smoke[216] before beginning the incantation, namely as soon as he lights the candles; he has to make it from the following, and light it for the spirits:

Frankincense[217]
Myrrh[218]
Mastic[219]
Rue[220]
Paradise wood[221]
Spermaceti[222]

---

216 Translator's note: Incense.

217 Translator's note: "Weyrauch" ("Weihrauch"), frankincense.

218 Translator's note: Myrrh is a gum-resin extracted from a number of small, thorny tree species of the genus *Commiphora*.

219 Translator's note: Mastic is a resin obtained from the mastic tree (*Pistacia lentiscus*). It is also known as "tears of Chios", being traditionally produced on the island Chios, and, like other natural resins, is produced in "tears" or droplets.

220 Translator's note: "Rauten". *Ruta graveolens*, known as rue, common rue, or herb-of-grace, is a species of *Ruta* grown as an ornamental plant and herb. It is native to the Balkan Peninsula.

221 Translator's note: "Paradies-Holtz", possibly meaning *Simarouba glauca*, otherwise known as paradise tree or bitter wood, an evergreen tree belonging to the *Quassia* family *Simaroubaceae*.

222 Original footnote: Spermaceti is a fatty and waxy substance from the head of the sperm whale, and is suitable for making candles.

This should be mixed together, then make a smoke of it; take as much of it as is necessary *ad fumigium*.[223]

But a little piece of paper must be wrapped around this light, on which are written the following words with a new pen and blood from a white dove, namely these words:

Jesus is my light.[224]

The exorcist must also have a little staff with him, which one is accustomed to calling the Staff of Carl.[225] This little staff must be without a blemish, a finger thick and a cubit long,[226] made from a hazelnut perennial,[227] and the exorcist must have this with him the circle. It must also have these four letters – J. N. R. J. – written on it

It is folly when some take a mere sword or dagger with them into the circle, as if they want to fight around with the spirits as with fencers, but nothing less. For we have to deal with spirits as princes of this world, who are driven out with nothing but the word of God, and other secret things. They fear little from the mere sword or loaded shot, but the one and only most holy word of Jesus, when it is spoken with true faith and pure heart, drives and haunts them, and puts them to flight.

The exorcist can also have three people with him, but they must have the same name; for example, the three must be called Johannes or have the name Christian; given names indeed have a special power in this work, for one can at once be reminded of his holy baptism—there can even be three Siegmunds in the circle, or

---

223 Translator's note: Latin, "for purposes of fumigating".

224 Translator's note: "Jesus ist mein Licht".

225 Translator's note: "Stab Caroli", i.e. the staff of Charlemagne.

226 Translator's note: "eines Fingers dick, und einer Elen lang". The cubit was an ancient unit of length based on the distance from the elbow to the middle finger.

227 Translator's note: "Haselnuß Stauden".

three Andräases; so that one lights the incense, the other makes the incantation, and the third pays attention to the lights and the smoke itself, with which he drives these evil spirits or devils from one another; this also represents the three, as the most perfect number.

In these three days, however, note that the exorcist with his companions must partake of the Holy Communion meal, and being sober, they must also not let a curse be heard from them for this time, otherwise they are in great danger. They must also practice the works of mercy towards the poor.

God is with us, who may be with us again.

Before we proceed to the circle, we wish to pull up a number of holy proverbs from sacred writ, with which the devils can be made to fear, when they want to bring us to some harm.

1.

The woman's seed shall crush the serpents' heads.

2.

Our God says, if your sins were red as blood, they shall become white as snow.[228]

3.

The blood of Jesus Christ, the Son of God, cleanses us from all sins.[229]

4.

Be of good cheer, my son, your sins are forgiven.[230]

---

228 Translator's note: See Isaiah 1:18.

229 Translator's note: See 1 John 1:7.

230 Translator's note: See Matthew 9:2.

5.
Jesus of Nazareth, a king of the Jews.[231]

6.
Jesus said to his disciples, if you have faith, you can move mountains.[232]

7.
My help comes from the Lord, who made heaven and earth.[233]

8.
The Lord keep me from all evil, the Lord keep my going out and coming in, from now until eternity.[234]

9.
I lift up my hands to you, who sits in heaven and rules the whole world.[235]

Now follows the circle in which the exorcist can sit or stand as he pleases, either alone or with his companions.[236]

---

231 Translator's note: See Mark 15:32.

232 Translator's note: See Matthew 17:20.

233 Translator's note: See Psalm 121:2.

234 Translator's note: See Psalm 121:7–8.

235 Translator's note: See Deuteronomy 32:40.

236 Translator's note: The Latin text in the image reads: "verbum carofactum est" (the word was made flesh) and "quxcung [read: quicunque] petieritis a patre in nomine meo dabit vobis" (whatsoever you ask of the father in my name, he will give to you".

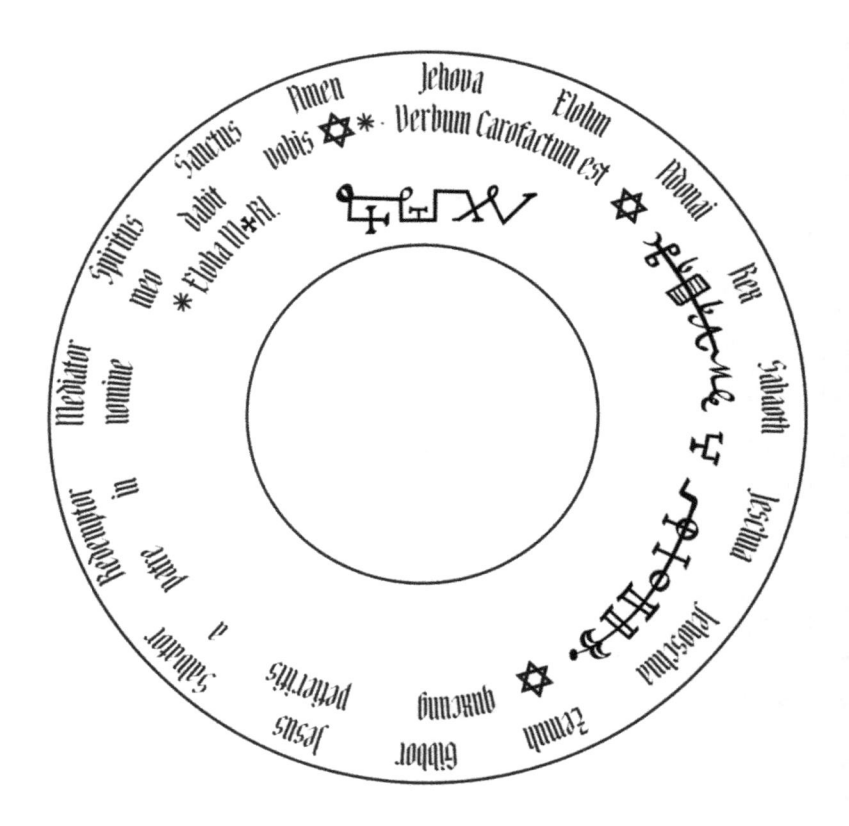

It is true that some write the names in the circle of even the foremost evil spirits; but it is ridiculous and against God's command, for so read the words: "I am the Lord your God, and after me there is no other"; it is rather dangerous if you have the name of the supreme devil in your circle, because you thereby concede to him a dominion over you. How do Christ and Belial rhyme together? You must admit that it is an open matter, however, that through sayings of Holy Scripture which are spoken in true faith, the evil spirits can be driven out; so do not trust the false devil's banners, which the wicked angels make of all kinds of figures and their characters in their circles, but rather put your trust in God.

When you have now prepared and finished everything as described above, and also acquired the above-mentioned smoking material, then light the incense and burn it in the circle, but with the incense [you should] recite the following prayer with devotion:

Lord God Sabaoth! You are a mighty king and ruler of the heavenly hosts! You who are the purest spirit. Bless this smoke, so that it may be a sweet smell; so the enemy of the soul of the human race and its trickery may not dare come into this circle; so that our intention be to give you praise and praise is given, now and forever, Amen.

This smoke must be lit in a new earthen vessel or pot which the exorcist must also take with him into the circle.[237]

You have to make the circles from new clean writing paper, and in doing so you have to be careful that you don't do anything with the spirits except under clear skies; and conjure during the waxing of the moon; for, as mentioned above the evil spirits[238] in cloudy and unfriendly weather are far more impetuous and stubborn than usual; they do appear, but I do not advise you to force them to appear at such a time.[239]

When the incantation actually takes place, all your thoughts and undertakings, under the designation of the Holy Cross, should take place in the name of the Holy Trinity through Jesus Christ. Amen.

When you step or walk into the circle, in the room or cellar, or under the open sky, where you want to do this work, do not undertake it before midnight; but the morning before, you have to wash and bathe your whole body; afterwards you should have

---

237 Translator's note: It is a classic tradition in magic ritual to use only a new earthen pot in which to burn incense or make various formulas for use in magical operations.

238 Translator's note: "die böse Geister".

239 Translator's note: For some reason, in *Zauber-Bibliothek* volume one, the text ends here (on page 156), but then it continues on in volume two (page 79). The remainder of the work is presented here, up to Psalm 91 at the end.

washed and put on clean clothes, especially your hereditary shirt; and at the same time wear the consecrated attachment piece as described above. You have to put on your head a pointed cap in the shape of a bishop's hat, made of beautiful delicate linen. The front part is surrounded with paper, on which the sacred name Tetragrammaton (the ineffable name of God) must be written. The place, however, must be cleaned of all uncleanliness and [it is to be] heavily smoked, but the paper or the headband around your hats must be formed and made thusly:[240]

These sacred letters must be written with the blood of a white dove, by means of a new and unused quill.

Incidentally, the exorcist can carry out the incantation alone, but if he takes someone with him, it is not so frightening; anyway, it is the case that three is a sacred number, so when there are three, one can carry the smoke, and that is two different [kinds of] incense; one is to soothe the spirits, and to lure them there; the other, to drive them away from it, which latter is only needed at the end.

He should also have a piece of chalk with him, so that he can make the following sign in addition to the circle in the four corners.

---

240 Original footnote: If the Tetragrammaton is to be on the hat, the "S" before the cross is to be a yod, i.e. the Hebrew letters Yod Heh Vau Heh.

THE HIDDEN AND TRUE PNEUMATOLOGY 63

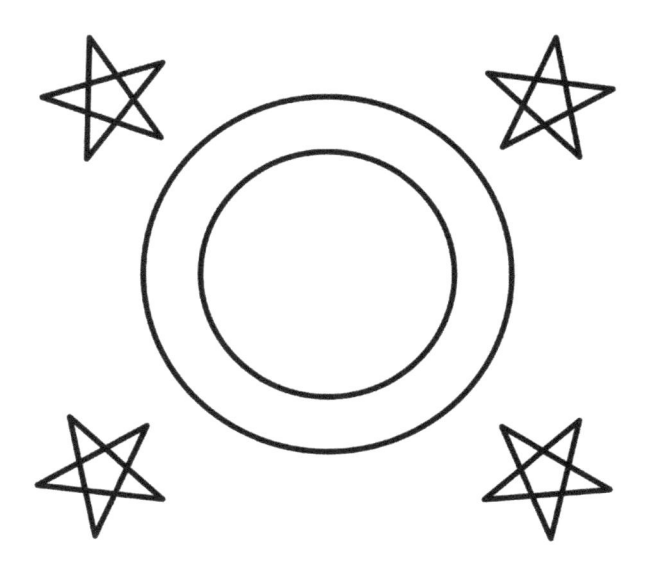

The other of the comrades can carry in one hand, two glasses with clear water; but in the other hand, mixed blood from a black lamb which is not a year old, and from a white dove, which is not yet two months old. They wear a crucifix, but the exorcist should walk with four wax lights, the Staff of Carl in the middle, and all three following in a row. The circle[241] should be wrapped around his body, around the navel and the chest; into the circle, however, [they] must go in the name of Jesus, who was crucified, died and rose again. Amen.

When he is in the usual place, he must take the circle off his body and lay it on the ground. His comrades must immediately enter and light the candles, and set them out as far as possible around one another. They can write the above-mentioned characters with the chalk outside of the circle; then the other mentioned blood and holy water must be sprinkled[242] outside of the circle. When

---
241 Translator's note: i.e., the paper on which it is drawn.
242 Translator's note: Or "sprayed".

this happens, they should fall on their knees, and everyone draw a cross on their forehead, mouth and breast, in the name of God the Father ✠ and the Son ✠ and the Holy Spirit. Amen.

After that, the comrades should stay back a little, but the exorcist, who has to be in the middle, should say the following prayer:

Almighty Lord God, our protector and strength for all those who hope in you; and protector of all those who are depressed and afflicted, including all who live in this house (or in this region). Be merciful to us, your servants, and shower upon us all your holy blessings at all times; so that we may be filled with your holiness through your grace, and be of good cheer. We beg you Lord, stand by us, help us in our affairs and bless the beginning, middle and end; so that our prayer and deed may have a happy ending, through your dear son, Jesus Christ our Lord, who is highly praised forever and ever. Amen.

Then one ignites the incense and the lights, under the name of the Holy Cross. When this has been done, you begin in the name of Jesus; and the evil spirits will then threaten and torment the poor soul, so that they resist the incantation.

☆

Then you have to speak up three times in a row and say: All good spirits praise the Lord God, who is with me (or with us).

Then the poor soul will sigh and weep, and speak in a hoarse voice: I too.

Then one continues speaking: I say to you and adjure you in the name of the crucified, dead and risen Jesus Christ; who atoned for all our sins, and also yours, on the trunk of the Cross; and [having] done enough, do not dare to oppose yourself to my (or our) charge, which we have begun to redeem you from roaming in the darknesses; and to bring you to rest until the day of judgment; but be still and hear what I ask of you; in the name of God the Father ✠ God the Son ✠ and God the Holy Spirit ✠ Amen.

Then make another smoke; the soul will then sigh again, but the guardians of the treasure will make a tumult and a fuss.

Regardless, you should keep speaking: You will be redeemed in the name of Jesus Christ, who is Gibbor, Yeshua, Jehoshua, our redeemer, the blessed seed of woman; before whose almighty name of Jesus, even the devil and all the damned spirits of hell will be afraid and tremble; and every knee bend which is in heaven, on earth, and under the earth, when you so desire. Then show the place where the treasure [that has] made you so miserable[243] is buried; so it may be an ointment on your head, in the name of Jesus, be praised forever.

The comrades of the exorcist then say: Amen.

Then the poor soul, on which side he is now standing, will indicate the place with tears and trembling; and will also indicate that he is bound by the guardians, and will be strictly held back; so bless him and make your incantation to the spirits.

Go in the name of Jesus Christ, who is your eternal salvation, in the name of the Holy Trinity of God the Father ✠ God the Son ✠ and God the Holy Spirit ✠. To this, the comrades reply: Amen.

At this point, the evil spirits will start [making] a horrible raven squawk, and croak like frogs; but do not be alarmed. Then you will be faced with many dazzling tricks,[244] so that you should stand back from your intentions. Ravens will fly around your head with a loud screech, and scare you with every imaginable fright; alone you shall trust only in God, and continue in the name of the Lord. But above all, you must have three pieces of bread with you, and three little pieces of paper on which the name of Jesus

---

243 Translator's note: "dich so unglückseelig gemacht".
244 Translator's note: "viele Blendungen und Gaucklereyen".

is written, because when they give you the treasure, you must immediately put the little pieces of paper with the pieces of bread on it, so they do not steal it away from you again, or transform [it] into something else, which they like to do when they can; for the spirits are frightfully malicious and deceitful.

Therefore, continue with the incantation thus: We are created in God's image; and by the grace of the Most High, of all human beings standing here, I conjure you in God's name; and invite you hellish spirits and princes, Acheront, Astharoth, Magoth, Asmodi, Beelzebub, Belial, Aimaymon, Paymon, Egym, with your subordinate custodians and servants, be you now whoever or whatever you will; and you present damned spirits, custodians and servants, through the most holy and almighty names of Jehovah, Adonay, Elohah, Saday and Samaoth, who is and was the God of Abraham, Isaac and Jacob; with whom also Moses spoke face to face on Mount Sinai, and who buried Moses himself; by he who dwells in the Holy of Holies, and by the Urim and Thumim[245] or the day and the night revealed his divine will, the very same most holy God is with us, you cursed spirits; and by the same I conjure you, that you obey my incantation and command; that you no longer guard this hidden treasure, but leave at this moment; namely in the strength and power of Tu Hagiu, Hagiotatu,[246] whom the holy angels adore; and in the heavens singing and crying out to all eternity: Holy! Holy! Holy! is the Lord Sabaoth. Now leave this place just as you had to quit the throne of the angels in heaven, such as you were, and never shall be again, you cursed and damned impure spirits! You shall no longer torment this poor soul; also you shall have no power to keep this treasure any longer, through the

---

245 Translator's note: In the Hebrew Bible, the Urim and the Thummim are elements of the hoshen, the breastplate worn by the High Priest attached to the ephod. They are connected with divination in general, and cleromancy in particular. Most scholars suspect that the phrase refers to a set of two objects used by the high priest to answer a question or reveal the will of God.

246 Translator's note: Transliterated Greek, "Holiest of Holies".

power and by command of Jesus Christ, the living Son of God, for all eternity. Amen.

Then they will reproach you,[247] [saying] you are far from being the one who is able to lift this treasure and redeem a poor soul. They will not only mock you and laugh, but also show all sorts of tricks, but you should answer them:

I know, you cursed spirits, that I am not able to do this of my own strength; but through the strength of Jesus Christ, who made me capable of this, of the seed of woman, who trampled on your head, deprived you of your principalities,[248] and triumphed over you. He has made me more holy through the bath of rebirth[249] and sealed me with his holy body and blood, when he suffered, was crucified and died for me, that I might live; but you are no longer the one who you were, as you have lost your former glory; therefore I charge you by this power which I possess, and by the one who made me powerful, who is Jesus of Nazareth, the living true Son of God.

I therefore conjure you again, to bring forth my treasure, in the name of Jesus; and pack yourselves off from here back to your damned hell,[250] where you are condemned and cast out for all eternity, through Jesus Christ, my Redeemer. Amen.

Here make the Holy Cross and make a smoke. After this, they will resist you anew in the greatest anger, and will hold all your sins against you, and drag all of your deeds and omissions through the barbs; only do not fear, as it is only a reprieve from the gallows for them.[251] They want you timid and afraid, so do not be led astray; therefore answer with the right trust in God, as follows, after you have once again signed yourself with the Holy

---

247 Translator's note: "hierauf werden sie dir fürwerffen".

248 Translator's note: "euch euer Fürstenthümer beraubet".

249 Translator's note: "durch das Baad der Wiedergeburth", the baptism.

250 Translator's note: "packet euch von hinnen in eure verdammte Hölle".

251 Translator's note: "dann es ist nur eine Galgenfrist bey ihnen".

Cross and made a smoke:

I am indeed a sinner, I confess that, but Jesus also atoned for my sins, he took them from me and freed me from them.

Then, with a devout heart, pray the following little prayer:

Oh you most holy God and man Jesus Christ! who are the true bread of heaven and food of angels. Also a terror of devils, who came from heaven into the world to bless it. Bow down with your grace to us and our need, even though we are full of sinful filth.[252] *We beg of you, let the merit of your holy suffering come to us through your grace. Be with us in this holy battle, so that we may be worthy of conquering ravenous wolves and stinking rams of hell; so that to you alone* ✠ *(Here make the sign of the Holy Cross) together with the Father* ✠ *and Holy* ✠ *Spirit, be praise and glory for all eternity, Amen.*

Now go and pack yourselves from here,[253] because Jesus is with us, you accursed spirits! You banished and damned mosquitoes, who seek to spoil the smell of loveliness; why do you tarry and hesitate any longer in vain? You know that Jesus has taken off your armor and deprived you of all power. Jesus is there, on whose breast John lay, who proclaimed the gospel:

In the beginning was the Word, and the Word was with God, and God was the Word. It was with God in the beginning, all things are made by it, and without it nothing was created. In it was life, and that life was the light of men; and the light shone in the darkness, and those of the darkness did not understand it. God sent a man whose name was John, who came to testify; that he should testify of the light, that all might believe through him. He was not of the light, but that he should bear witness to the light. It was a true light that enlightens all men who come into this world. It was in the world and the world was made by it, but the world did not recognize it. He came into his property, and it did not receive him; but as many as did receive him, to those he gave power to become children of God; specifically those who believe in his name, who

---

252 Translator's note: "ob wir gleich voll sündlichen Unflaths seyn".

253 Translator's note: "nun trollet und packet euch von hinnen".

are not born of blood, nor of the will of the flesh, nor of the will of man, but born of God. And the Word became flesh and dwelt among us; and we have seen his glory. The glory of the Son of the Father, full of grace and truth.

Jesus, the inseparable Word of the Father, is here; who rises eternally from the Father, and reigns with Him. Jesus is present, the splendor of fatherly glory; and all earthly and hellish knees must bow before his image; and all tongues confess that Jesus Christ is Lord, to the glory of God the Father.

Jesus is here, King of Kings and Lord of Lords, whose kingdom is not food and drink, but righteousness, peace and joy in the Holy Spirit; whose kingdom and power and glory are eternal.

Jesus is here, who is in one flesh, God and man, and the one Christ, whom neither the sea, nor the earth, nor the heavens of all heavens can comprehend.

Jesus is here, who refreshes those oppressed and burdened by sin, and gives rest to weary souls.

Jesus is here, who does not flee from all the ravenous wolves, but lays down his life for his sheep.

Jesus is here, who on his authority, commands the unclean spirits to obey him; who in the Jewish school,[254] drove out the devil from a man, which cried out: What do I have to do with you, Jesus of Nazareth, you came here to torment me.[255]

Jesus is here, who admonished us to fight again, and has brought about victory through this; and through all this, we bind you, we conjure and we compel you, cursed creatures, who for your arrogance were damned and cast out by God Almighty, that you pack yourselves up and go to your hellish dwelling, where you belong; to your torment which lasts for all eternity.

And now make another smoke, and if they want to stay longer, show them the signs written on paper with pigeon blood, like so:

---

254 Translator's note: "der Judenschule".

255 Translator's note: "du bist gekommen mich zu quälen".

PNEUMATOLOGIA OCCULTA ET VERA

Final Incantation

After this, proceed to the following final incantation:

In the name of God the Father ✠ of the Son ✠ and of the Holy Spirit ✠ Amen.

Hel ✠ Heloym ✠ Sother ✠ Emmanuel ✠ Sabaoth ✠ Agla ✠ Tetragrammaton ✠ Agyros ✠ Otheos ✠ Ishyros ✠ Athanatos ✠ Jehovah ✠ Va ✠ Adonay ✠ Saday ✠ Homousion ✠ Messiah ✠ Eschereheye ✠

Uncreated Father ✠
Uncreated Son ✠
Uncreated Holy Spirit ✠
Jesus Christ victorious ✠[256]
Christ reigns ✠[257]
Christ rules ✠[258]

If you are now a sinful soul, NN. [name] (here turn to the poor soul and continue speaking), the devil binding you, or otherwise tempting you and overwhelming you in some way, so it is for you, through this power and through his merit and great mercy Jesus Christ, the living Son of God, who came from heaven and into the immaculate body of the holy Virgin Mary for the salvation of men, and to destroy the devil's kingdom, [that] man becomes free from all unclean spirits, and all devils are chased away from you, and into the bottomless abyss of hell; behold the Lord's Cross and your enemies flee; the lion of the tribe of Judah and the root of

---

[256] Translator's note: "Jesus Christus sieget".
[257] Translator's note: "Christus regieret".
[258] Translator's note: "Christus herrschet".

David has conquered; therefore I command and order you, and we together command and order you devils and all cursed spirits, whatever name you may have, that you give up all power over us and this treasure; this we command and order you, through the coming of Jesus Christ, and through his holy birth, for it is said:

A child is born to us; a child is given to us whose dominion is on his shoulder; through his innocent death, and his innocent blood, which he shed on the wood of the cross for us.

Note: Here [the exorcist] shows them the cross and the image of the crucified Jesus Christ, and speaks:

I conjure and command you again, you wicked and cursed hellhounds,[259] depart from us and this treasure; into the dark forests and unclean puddles, and into the raging river in hell,[260] and I command you through the five holy wounds of Jesus Christ; but we commend ourselves, and this treasure, to the almighty mercy of God Almighty, and of his son, our dear Lord Jesus Christ.

I conjure and bind you, all you accursed spirits; leave us and this treasure through the power of divine salvation, who is Jehovah, the living God; through the crucified and crowned God, from before whose holy face you are cast out; and through God's death and burial; and through the victorious resurrection of God, who went down to hell and triumphed over you; who is the true God and true man.

I adjure you by all the gospels that are read and preached throughout the Christian world, and by the holy Ten Commandments, which God Himself wrote on Mount Sinai with his holy finger; and by the twelve articles of Christian faith;[261] and by the holy cross on which Jesus Christ redeemed the whole world and human race from the power of your prince, Sathanae.

---

259 Translator's note: "Höllenhunde".

260 Translator's note: "in die düstre Wälder un unreine Pfützschen, und in den tobenden Höllenfluß".

261 Translator's note: See Appendix C.

I implore you by the glorious ascension of Jesus Christ, you accursed hellish crowds; leave us and this treasure, which you have held until now. Don't transform and dislocate it; still less do harm to us in either body or soul, nor to everything we have. Nor defile this circle in which we are, by the power of Jesus Christ, who has come to judge the quick and the dead,[262] and to damn you into the abyss of hell for ever; bring the treasure and then flee from us, by the power of your judge Jesus Christ. In the name of God the Father ✠ God the Son ✠ and God the Holy Spirit ✠ Amen.

This must be repeated three times.

After that, make the following smoke to drive away the devils.

Sulfur[263]
Devil dirt[264]
Castoreum[265]
Rue[266]

Grind these together and made an incense with them.

Then they will bring the treasure and the vessel, inside which is the same, with the greatest malice, rage and impetuosity, and also with terrible threats, to you in the circle, and make a noise as if everything is about to collapse, and an earthquake is coming.

---

262 Translator's note: "the quick and the dead", an idiomatic phrase introduced by early English translations of the New Testament, is mentioned also in *The Secret Grimoire of Turiel* by Marius Malchus, Weiser/Aquarian Press, 1960, where it is stated on page 31, "Holy, Holy, Holy, Lord God of Sabaoth, which will come to judge the quick and the dead. Thou art Alpha and Omega, the first and the last".

263 Translator's note: "Schwefel".

264 Translator's note: "Teufelsdreck". Possibly Asafoetida, the dried latex (gum oleoresin) exuded from the rhizome or tap root of several species of Ferula.

265 Translator's note: "Bibergeil". This is a reference to castoreum, a compound that is produced by a beaver's castor sacs, which, while they're located in the same vicinity, are not the same thing as anal glands.

266 Translator's note: "Rauten". Probably rue, as was previously used in another incense.

Now, as soon as they have brought it in, throw the three pieces of bread and paper upon it, so that they cannot dare to remove it or transform it; and take care not to touch it with your hand or finger before it stands for at least half an hour, and then the spirits will leave. If they don't want to leave, then make the aforementioned smoke again; then they will leave behind such a stench that your smoke won't bother them. They will make a cruel banging, and this is the sign of their leaving; but your comrades therefore may not yet speak before the exorcist has made a prayer to God, and thanks have been given to the poor soul, who must also be blessed.

Therefore, each one prays a holy Our Father,[267] quietly and with raised hands, etc.

After that, the exorcist must say the following prayer with a loud voice and great devotion in their heart:

O, you holy threefold God, Father ✠ Son ✠ and Holy ✠ Spirit, thanks unto you now and forever, for you have dignified us to free this poor soul from the power of the devil, that he may now rest until the Day of Judgment; we also thank you, for your mercy has preserved us fro the power of the rending, hellish Wolf and his followers. You merciful Father of our Lord Jesus Christ, now further grant this poor soul the grace, that he may serve you in eternal salvation and praise your mercy through Jesus Christ, who redeemed him upon the trunk of the Cross for all eternity. Amen.

But you, redeemed soul! praise and glorify with us God the Father, almighty creator of heaven and earth; now go in peace and leave this place, in the name of Jesus Christ, who is our redeemer and yours; whose dear blood was shed for your sins. May he bless you and be merciful to you on the day of the coming judgment, so that you may be numbered among the elect, and reckoned among the blessed and holy angels, through Jesus Christ. Amen.

All good spirits praise the Lord God with us.

---

267 Translator's note: i.e., the Lord's Prayer.

Then make the sign of the Holy Cross, and smoke with the fragrant incense which was recorded and written above.

At this the soul will extend his hands to you in thanksgiving; but be careful not to join hands, otherwise you will be horribly burned, especially if he still feels anything of his previous torment; but instead extend the Staff of Carl, on which you will then find a clear mark or sign of burning; after which he will go away sighing with perfect contentment, when you have previously blessed him with the sign of the Holy Cross, and with renewed fragrant incense.

Now everyone prays in silence and with a devout heart the holy Our Father, etc. But after that, all togeth with a loud voice:

91st Psalm.[268]

Whoever dwells in the secret place of the Most High will remain under the shield of God.

He will say to the Lord, It is you who receives me and in my refuge, my God, I trust in you.

Then he freed me from the snare of the hunters, and from harsh words.

He will cover you with his arms and you will have hope under his wings.

His truth will put a shield around you. You will not be afraid before the terrors of the night.

Before the arrow that flies in the day, before the sickness that roams in the dark, before the destruction at noon time.

A thousand will fall at your side, and ten thousand at your right hand, but will not come near to you.

But you will behold with your eyes and see the vengeance of the wicked.

---

268 Translator's note: See Appendix C.

Then Lord you are my confidence, you have set the Most High as your refuge.

No misfortune will come to you, and the plague will not come near your dwellings.

Then he commanded his angels to protect you in all your ways; they will carry you in their hands so that you do not stumble your foot on a stone.

Thou shalt walk upon adders and basilisks, and trample the lions and dragons.

Because he had hope in me, I will deliver him, I will protect him, for he has known my name.

He will call to me and I will hear him, I am with him in tribulation, I will save him and bring him honor.

I will satisfy him with long life and show him my salvation.

Glory be to God the Father ✠ and the Son ✠ and the Holy Spirit ✠, as He was in the beginning, now and forever, Amen.

Appendix A

GLOSSARY OF NAMES OF THE ANGELS, SPIRITS AND SELECTED GOD-NAMES LISTED IN THIS BOOK
(IN THE ORDER THEY APPEAR IN THE TEXT)

Hecate: Or Hekate, is a goddess of ancient Greek mythology, often represented as holding snakes, a key, a pair of torches, accompanied by dogs, etc.; in later periods, as a lunar goddess depicted in triple form, representing the lunar stages of new moon, full moon and dark moon.

Zebaoth: Or Sabaoth or Tzevaot, a name of God in the Hebrew tradition, "the hosts of heaven" in the biblical title "Lord (God) of Sabaoth". The name Sabaoth also appears in the Old Testament in reference to an army. In the First Book of Samuel, the name is used as a name of God. In Gnostic texts, the name is evidently rendered as "over all the forces (of chaos)".

Aratron, **Bethor**, **Phaleg**, **Och**, **Hagith**, **Ophiel**, and **Phuel**: The seven Olympic spirits, also known as the "stewards of heaven". (see *A Dictionary of Angels* by Gustav Davidson. Also, see *Arbatel of Magic* and *The Secret Grimoire of Turiel*.)

Aratron: First of the Olympian spirits, governing over the planet Saturn, and rules over 49 of 196 Olympic provinces. He teaches alchemy, magic and medicine.

Bethor: Rules over 42 Olympic regions, and governs over the planet Jupiter.

Phaleg: Or Phalec, rules over 35 Olympic regions, and governs over the planet Mars. Agrippa refers to him as the "war lord".

Och: Rules over 28 Olympic regions, governs over the Sun, and is described as a "prince of alchemy".

Hagith: Rules over either 21 or 35 Olympic regions, and governs over the planet Venus.

Ophiel: Governs over the planet Mercury; his name appears on the Necromantic Bell of Girardius, which is rung to summon the dead (see *Arbatel of Magic*).

Phuel: Or Phul, governs over the Moon, and is called "lord of the Moon and supreme lord of the waters".

Michael: "Who is like God", chief of the order of Virtues, considered one of the greatest of all angels, also chief of archangels; was worshiped as something of a god by the Chaldeans. A full book could be composed regarding the mythology of the angel Michael.

Leviathan: In rabbinical writings, Leviathan is identified with Rahab, the angel of the primordial deep, and associated with Behemoth. In the Enoch parables, Leviathan is the primitive female "sea dragon" and the monster of evil.

Adonai, Jehovah, Eloha, Alph, Ben, Ruach-Hachedosch, Elohim, Adonai, Zebaoth, Messiah, Soter, Emanuel, Agla, Tetragrammaton: Hebrew names of God used for the "divine rod".

Adonai: Hebrew name of God used most commonly in modern prayer, defined as "the light of the Lord".

Agla: Hebrew name of God, actually an acronym, being Atha Gibor La'olam Adonai, translated as "Thou the Lord, are mighty forever".

Elohim: Hebrew name for God, meaning "supreme one" or "mighty one". Grammatically plural name for God (El).

Tetragrammaton: Hebrew name of God, its meaning is "consisting of four letters", or tetragram, that is the four-letter Hebrew name Yod Heh Vau He.

Ariel: "The Lion of God", he ranks as one of seven princes who rules the waters, and is "Earth's great Lord" (see *Hierarchie of the Blessed Angells* by Thomas Heywood.)

Agiel: Saturn's Intelligence.

Zazel: Spirit or Demon of Saturn.

Johphiel: Jupiter's Intelligence.

Hismael: Spirit or Demon of Jupiter.

Graphiel: Mars's Intelligence.

Barzabel: Spirit or Demon of Mars.

Nachiel: The Sun's Intelligence.

Sorath: Spirit or Demon of the Sun.

Hagiel: Venus's Intelligence.

Kedemel: Spirit or Demon of Venus.

Bne Seraphim: Venus's Intelligences.

Tiriel: Mercury's Intelligence.

Taphthartharath: Spirit or Demon of the Mercury.

Hasmodai: Spirit or Demon of the Moon.

Schedbarschemoth Schartathan: Spirit of Spirits of the Moon.

Malcha betharsithim hed beruah schehakim: Intelligency of the Intelligence of the Moon.

Metatron: The first (and the last) of the ten archangels of the Briatic world. Again, a large book could be composed regarding the angel of this name. (see *A Dictionary of Angels*, *Jewish Magic and Superstition* by Joshua Trachtenberg, *The Zohar*, etc.)

Orphaniel: Ruler of the first legion, his planet is the Moon, and he is invoked in Monday conjurations. (See *The Secret Grimoire of Turiel*.)

Zaphiel: Ruler of the order of Cherubim, prince of the planet Saturn, and the preceptor Angel of Noah.

Camael: "He who sees God", chief of the order of Powers, and one of the archangels of the Briatic world.

Raphael: One of the three great archangels (with Michael and Gabriel) of post-Biblical lore, there are numerous biblical legends involving Raphael and Abraham, Jacob, Noah, etc.

Haniel: "Glory (or Grace) of God", he is angel of the month of December, and chief of the order of Principalities, virtues and innocents. (See *The Magus, or Celestial Intelligencer* by Francis Barrett.)

Michael: See above.

Gabriel: "God is my strength", angel of January, ruler over Aquarius; again, there are so many references to the angel Gabriel that full volumes might be composed.

Machidiel: "Fullness of God", governing angel of the month of March, ruler of the sign of Aries.

Aomodel: Should be Asmodel, ruler of the sign of Taurus, governing angel of the month of April.

Ambriel: Angel of the month of May, and prince of the order of Thrones, ruler of the sign of Gemini.

(**Muriel**, missing from the list in the book, is the angel of the month of June, and ruler over the sign of Cancer.)

Verchiel: Also known as Varchiel, angel of July, and ruler over Leo.

Hamabiel: Should be Hamaliel, angel of August, ruler over Virgo. (see *Hierarchie of the Blessed Angells* by Heywood.)

Zuriel: Also known as Uriel, angel of September, ruler over Libra.

Barbiel: Angel of the month October, ruler over Scorpio. (see *The Magus* by Barrett.)

Annachiel: Should be Advachiel or Adnachiel, angel of November, ruler over Sagittarius. Annachiel is actually the angel governing over the planet Saturn; also see the third pentacle of Saturn in the *Key of Solomon* by MacGregor Mathers.

Hannael: Angel of December, ruler over Capricorn; also see Haniel above.

Barchiel: Angel of February, ruler over Pisces. Also known as Barakiel.

Beelzebub: A name derived from the title of a Philistine god, formerly worshiped in Ekron, and later adopted by some Abrahamic religions as a major demon. The name Beelzebub is associated with the Canaanite god Baal, and in Christian theology, another name for Satan. There are numerous myths and legends regarding Beelzebub, most familiar as "the lord of flies"; see *A Dictionary of Angels* by Davidson.

Ahab: Ahab was the seventh king of Israel, the son and successor of King Omri and the husband of Jezebel of Sidon, according to the Hebrew Bible [1 Kings 16:29–34]. The Bible portrays Ahab as a wicked king, particularly for condoning Jezebel's influence on religious policies and his principal role in Naboth's arbitrary execution. The existence of Ahab is historically supported outside the Bible; Shalmaneser III of Assyria documented in 853 BCE that he defeated an alliance of a dozen kings in the Battle of Qarqar, one of these being Ahab. He is also mentioned in the inscriptions of the Mesha Stele. Ahab became king of Israel in the thirty-eighth year of King Asa of Judah, and reigned for twenty-two years, according to 1 Kings 16:29. William F. Albright dated his reign to 869–850 BCE, while Edwin R. Thiele offered the dates 874–853 BCE. Most recently, Michael Coogan has dated Ahab's reign to 871–852 BCE.

Apollo: Apollo is one of the Olympian deities in classical Greek and Roman religion and mythology. The national divinity of the Greeks, Apollo has been recognized as a god of archery, music and dance, truth and prophecy, healing and diseases, the Sun and light, poetry, and more. One of the most important and complex of the Greek gods, he is the son of Zeus and Leto, and the twin brother of Artemis, goddess of the hunt.

Pythian spirit and the **Pythonic Woman**: From the *International Standard Bible Encyclopedia* entry for "Python":

> Occurs only in Acts 16:16, where the Revised Version (British and American) reads, "a certain maid having a spirit of divination [margin: "a spirit, a Python"] met us." Puthon, or Putho, is the oldest name of Delphi (or the country about Delphi), in which was situated the famous Delphic Oracle. Consequently "Pythian spirit" came to be the generic title of the supposed source of inspiration of diviners, including the slave-girl of the account in Acts. Exactly what facts underlie the narrative it is rather hard to say, but it is evident that the girl was sincere in her conviction that she spoke with Pythian inspiration. Probably she represents some hysterical type, of none too strong mentality, whose confused utterances were taken

as coming from some supernatural power. Impressed by Paul's personality, she followed him about, and, when his command came, was in a state of mind that had prepared her to obey it. The narrative, incidentally, gives an interesting sidelight on a society in which a girl with hysteria had a greater commercial value than she had after her cure.[269]

The Bible also says about the spirits of Python (Leviticus 20:27): "And if there be a man or a woman in whom is a spirit of Python or of divination, they shall certainly be put to death: they shall stone them with stones; their blood is upon them." (or "a charmer", or "one that inquireth of a spirit of Python", or "a soothsayer", or "one that consulteth the dead").

Belial: Belial is the 68th spirit of the Goetia, considered a "demon king". In Hebrew, *belial* is a word "used to characterize the wicked or worthless". There are many references to Belial in various texts, including a German work entitled *Das Buch Belial*, by Jacobus de Teramo, published in Augsberg, 1473.

Tobias: Tobit, The Book of Tobit, which is also known as the Book of Tobias or the Book of Tobi, from the early second century BCE, a Hebrew text describing how God tests the faithful, and responds to prayers, protecting the Israelites. It tells the tale of two Jewish families, one of the blind Tobit in Nineveh and secondly the abandoned Sarah in Ecbatana. Tobit's son Tobias is sent to acquire ten silver talents which Tobit had left in a town in Media named Rages. He was guided and assisted by the angel Raphael. He reaches Ecbatana and meets Sarah there, but a spirit named Asmodeus has already fallen in love

---

269 "Python', The International Standard Bible Encyclopedia <https://www.internationalstandardbible.com/P/python.html>.

with her, and he kills anyone she intends to marry. However, with the aid of Raphael, the demon is exorcised, so Tobias and Sarah then marry, after which they return to Nineveh where Tobit is cured of his blindness.

Asmodeus: Spellings range from Asmadai, to Asmoday, Asmodee, Chammaday, etc. Asmodeus is the 32nd spirit of the Goetia, considered a "demon king". There are numerous references to him in various texts, including *The Magus* by Barrett, *Dictionnaire Infernal* by De Plancy, and the *Book of Abramelin*.

Sathan: Variant spelling of Satan, of which there are volumes written.

Meierim: Or Meririm, identified as the evil power whom Paul in Ephesians describes as "prince of the power of the air" (i.e. Satan). See *The Magus* by Barrett, who claims he is a prince over the angels of Revelation. Also see *Three Books of Occult Philosophy*.

Abaddon: "Destroyer", the Hebrew name for the Greek Apollyon, "angel of the bottomless pit", as in Revelation 9:10; also the angel (or star) that binds Satan for 1000 years, in Revelation 20. In the *Key of Solomon*, Abaddon is a name for God that Moses invoked to bring down the blighting rain over Egypt. There are numerous reference to this name in various texts on Hebrew mythology.

Astaroth: Astaroth is the 29th spirit of the Goetia, and the Great Duke of Hell in the first hierarchy with Beelzebub and Lucifer; he is part of the evil trinity. He is a male figure most likely named after the Near Eastern goddess Astarte. In John Bunyan's *Holy War*, Diabolus is a name of Astaroth, and he was aided in the war against Shaddai (God) by Apollyon, Python, Cerberus, Legion, Lucifer, and other "diabolonians".

Mamon: Mammon is described as a fallen angel now ruling in hell, and in *Dictionnaire Infernal* by Colin de Plancy, is certified as "Hell's ambassador to England".

Lucifer: "Light-giver", often mistakenly compared with the fallen angel Satan. There are numerous references to Lucifer in various works, notably the Old Testament, and Milton's *Paradise Lost*.

Aetus: Or Aeeta, was a king of Colchis in Greek mythology, and one of the Telchines. The name comes from the ancient Greek word αἰετός or aietós, meaning "eagle". Aeëtes was the son of the Sun god Helios and the Oceanid Perseis, brother of Circe, Perses and Pasiphaë, and father of Medea, Chalciope and Absyrtus.

Megalosius: Or Megalesius. One of the Telchines, a family, class of people, or tribe, said to have been descended from Thalassa or Poseidon. The following are mentioned as the names of individual Telchines: Mylas, Atabyrius, Antaeus, Megalesius, Hormenus, Lycus, Nicon, Simon, Chryson, Argyron, Chalcon. (see *Bulfinch's Mythology* and *The Magus* by Barrett.)

Ormenus: In Greek mythology, Ormenus or Ormenos is the name of several different men, but specifically is one of the Telchines.

Lycus: Name of one of the Telchines. Also, Lycus was the name of a son of Ares who was a Libyan king that sacrificed strangers to his father. He was also the father of Callirhoê, who rescued Diomedes from being sacrificed, and committed suicide upon his departure.

Kyeon: Some version of a Telchine name, probably Nycon.

Minos: One of the Telchines, probably Mimon. Also In Greek mythology, Minos was a king of Crete, son of Zeus and Europa. Every nine years, he made King Aegeus pick seven young boys and seven young girls to be sent to Daedalus's creation, the labyrinth, to be eaten by the Minotaur.

Saturnus: The Roman god of agriculture and farming.

Michael, **Raphael**, **Gabriel**, **Uriel**: The four archangels.

Seraph: An angel governing the element of fire. Singular of Seraphim. See *Hierarchie of the Bleesed Angells* by Heywood.

Cherub: An angel governing the element of air. Singular of Cherubim. See *Key of Solomon*.

Tharsis: An angel governing the element of water. See *Hierarchie of the Blessed Angells* by Heywood.

Samael: In rabbinic literature, chief of the satans and the angel of death. In the Book of Enoch, the prince of demons. Also, see *Three Books of Occult Philosophy* by Agrippa.

Alzazel: Also known as Azazel, Azaziel, "God Strengthens", one of the chiefs of the 200 fallen angels (Revelation speaks of one third of the heavenly host being involved in the fall). See the Book of Enoch.

Azael: Sometimes identified with Alzazel; in *Dictionnaire Infernal* by De Plancy, Azael is chained in a desert until the day of judgment. Also, see *Three Books of Occult Philosophy* by Agrippa.

Machazael: Or Machasiel, one of the angels invoked from the south, residing in the fourth heaven, and listed as one of the intelligences of the Sun. See *The Secret Grimoire of Turiel*, *Heptameron* and Barrett's *The Magus*.

Astharoth: See Astaroth above. Also, see *The Book of Abramelin* re: the eight demon princes.

Magoth: Or Maguth, an angel of the air operating on Thursday, minister to the south, chief of the air angels. See *The Book of Abramelin* re: the eight demon princes. Also see *Heptameron*, and *The Magus* by Barrett.

Asmodi: See Asmodeus above. Also, see *The Book of Abramelin* re: the eight demon princes.

Oriens: One of the four demons overseeing the cardinal directions. The Latin root of his name suggests that Oriens is the infernal king of the east. See *The Book of Abramelin*.

Paymon: Or Paimon, an angel of the order of Dominions prior to the fall, but in hell he is a great king obedient to Lucifer. Also, see *The Book of Abramelin*, re: the eight demon princes, and *Dictionnaire Infernal* by De Plancy.

Ariton: Also known as Egin or Egyn, a demonic sub-prince with dominion over water. He is named as one of the four demons who presides over the cardinal directions. See *The Book of Abramelin* re: the eight demon princes, *Dictionnaire Infernal* by De Plancy, and *The Magus* by Barrett.

Amaymon: Is said to know the past, present, and future. He can enable visions and allow people to fly; he provides familiar spirits and causes others to emerge in diverse forms; and, he summons protection and revives the dead. He is also identified as one of the four infernal rulers of the cardinal directions, his direction being south. See *The Book of Abramelin*.

Egyn: See Ariton above.

Dardiel: Or Dardael, one of three angels of the Lord's day. See *The Magus* by Barrett, and *Heptameron*.

Hurtapel: Another of the three angels of the Lord's day, along with Michael. See *The Magus* by Barrett, and *Heptameron*.

Varcan: King of angels of the air ruling the Lord's day; see *Heptameron*. Also, an angel with dominion over the Sun. See *Hierarchie of the Blessed Angells* by Heywood.

Arcan: King of the angels of the air, ruler of Monday. See *The Magus* by Barrett.

Zephyrus: Angel of the west wind.

Satael: Angel of the air and of Tuesday, also presiding spirit of the planet Mars. See *The Magus* and *Heptameron*.

Amaliel: Or Amabiel, an angel of the air on Tuesday, and presiding spirit of Mars; description appears identical to Satael. Also mentioned in both *The Magus* and *Heptameron*, as well as *The Secret Grimoire of Turiel*.

Samex: Also Samax, an angel of the air and ruling over Tuesday. See *The Magus* and *Heptameron*.

Subsolanus: Or Solanus, the angel of the east wind, the name meaning "lying beneath the sun", the wind that comes from the rising sun. Also known in Greek as Apeliotes.

Miel: Angel of Wednesday, one of three angels presiding over the planet Mercury. See *Heptameron*.

Saraphiel: Or Seraphiel, another presiding angel of Mercury, ruling on Tuesday, and invoked from the north. See also *The Magus* and *The Secret Grimoire of Turiel*.

Medial: Or Modial the king, one of the guardians of the gate of the east wind.

Africus: Of the south west wind, the sirocco wind, named because it blew off the coast of Africa.

Sachiel: "Covering of God". This angel is a bit contradictory, as he is known to be an angel of Monday, and invoked from the south, but also as an angel of Thursday and invoked from the west. Also, a presiding spirit of Jupiter. This name is also represented in the "Goetia", and see *The Magus*.

Castael: Or Castiel, an angel of Thursday. Also possibly Cassiel, one of the rulers of Saturn, in the order of Powers, and one of three angels of Saturday. There is also contradictory information presented for this angel.

Asasiel: Angel of Thursday, with Sachiel and Cassiel, and one of the presiding spirits of Jupiter. See *The Magus*, *Heptameron* and *The Secret Grimoire of Turiel*.

Suth: The angel of air is called Suth the king.

Auster: The south wind. The embodiment of the sirocco wind, a southerly wind which brings cloudy weather, powerful winds and rain to southern Europe.

Anael: Angel ruling over Friday, and has dominion over Venus. See *Three Books of Occult Philosophy* by Agrippa, and *Heptameron*, etc.

Rachiel: One of the presiding spirits of Venus, one of three angels of Friday. See *The Magus*, and *Three Books of Occult Philosophy* by Agrippa.

Sarabotref: An angel of the air on Friday.

Cassiel: See Castael above.

Machatan: Or Machator or Macoton, angel of Saturday, one of the powers of the spirits of the air, ruling with Uriel, Cassiel and Seraquiel. See *The Magus*.

Uriel: See Zuriel above.

Maymon: See Amaymon above.

Afrus: The southwest wind.

Acheront: Possibly Achartiel, Achtariel, Acrabiel, Aker, Akteriel etc.; see *A Dictionary of Angels* by Davidson. Name possibly influenced by the infernal river Acheron in Greek myth.

Various divine names of God in the text, many of Hebrew origin: Hel, Helomy, Sother, Emmanuel, Sabaoth, Agla, Tetragrammaton, Agyros, Otheos, Ishyros, Athanatos, Jehovah, Va, Adonay, Saday, Homousion, Messiah, Eschereheye.

Appendix B

A Selection of Treasure Spells In Various Grimoire Texts

From ***Grimorium Verum*** (translation by Joseph Peterson, CreateSpace Publishing, 2007):

For Discovering Treasures

Go to the place where you suspect there is a treasure, and say, striking three times with the heel of the left foot against the earth, and turning around on the left:

Sadies, Satani, Agir fons toribus come to me. Saradon, who will be called Sarietuur.

Repeat three times in a row. And if there is any treasure in this place you will know it, because a voice will tell you in your ear.

From ***The Black Books of Elverum*** (translation by Mary Rustad, Galde Press, 1999):

Swearing Over a Divining Rod

"I (name), beseech you, noble stick, in the name of the Father, the Son, and the Holy Spirit, that you truthfully show me, point out, and guide me to the place where there is gold, silver, or money, which has been made by human hands and is hidden in the earth. Be as true as the Virgin Mary was a pure virgin, before and after the birth of Christ." So certain and true as Christ is the son of God, and so certain and true as God's son died for man's sins and is all mankind's savior. I beseech you, stick, with your might and power as Jesus conquered the Devil and all evil spirits and made them most humble. I beseech you, stick, that you alone point out old treasures which are hidden by man, and not any other minerals or metals. Continue looking when you are commanded. With God's holy gospel, His holy word, with the angels, the martyrs, the Devil's downfall and confinement, and with the loud trumpet's sound that on the day of judgement shall give life to all nature's dead and living.

From ***The Key of Solomon the King*** (translation by S.L. MacGregor Mathers, London: George Redway, 1889):
How to Render Thyself Master of a Treasure Possessed by the Spirits
The Earth being inhabited, as I have before said unto thee, by a great number of Celestial Beings and Spirits, who by their subtilty and prevision know the places wherein treasures are hidden, and seeing that it often happeneth that those men who undertake a search for these said treasures are molested and sometimes put to death by the aforesaid Spirits, which are called Gnomes; which, however, is not done through the Avarice of these said Gnomes, a Spirit being incapable of possessing anything, having no material senses wherewith to bring it into use, but because these Spirits, who are enemies of the passions, are equally so of Avarice, unto which men are so much inclined; and foreseeing the evil ends for which these treasures will be employed have some interest and aim in maintaining the earth in its condition of price and value, seeing that they are its inhabitants, and when they slightly disturb the workers in such kind of treasures, it is a warning which they give them to cease from the work, and if it happen that the greedy importunity of the aforesaid workers oblige them to continue, notwithstanding the aforesaid warnings, the Spirits, irritated by their despising the same, frequently put the workmen to death. But know, O my Son, that from the time that thou shalt have the good fortune to be familiar with such kinds of Spirits, and that thou shalt be able by means of what I have taught thee to make them submit unto thine orders, they will be happy to give thee, and to make thee partaker in that which they uselessly possess, provided that thine object and end shall be to make a good use thereof.

The Manner of Performing the Operation: On a Sunday before sunrise, between the 10th of July and the 20th of August, when the moon is in the Sign of the Lion, thou shalt go unto the place where thou shalt know either by interrogation of the Intelligences, or otherwise, that there is a treasure; there thou shalt describe a Circle of sufficient size with the Sword of Magical Art wherein to open up the earth, as the nature of the ground will allow; thrice during the day shalt thou cense it with the incense proper for the day, after which being clothed in the raiment proper for the Operation thou shalt suspend in some way by a machine immediately above the opening a lamp, whose oil should be mingled with the fat of a man who has died in the month of July, and the wick being made from the cloth wherein he has been buried. Having kindled this with fresh fire, thou shalt fortify the workmen with a girdle of the skin of a goat newly slain, whereon shall be written with the blood of the dead man from whom thou shalt have taken the fat these words and characters; and thou shalt set them to work in safety, warning them not to be at all disturbed at the Spectres which they will see, but to work away boldly. In case they cannot finish the work in a single day, every time they shall have to leave it thou shalt cause them to put a covering of wood over the opening, and above the covering about six inches of earth; and thus shalt thou continue unto the end, being all the time present in the raiment of the Art, and with the Magic Sword, during the operation. After which thou shalt repeat this prayer

Prayer: ADONAI, ELOHIM, EL, EHEIEH ASHER EHEIEH, Prince of Princes, Existence of Existences, have mercy upon me, and cast Thine eyes upon Thy Servant (N.), who invokes Thee most devoutedly, and supplicates Thee by Thy Holy and tremendous Name Tetragrammaton to be propitious, and to order Thine Angels and Spirits to come and take up their abode in this place; O ye Angels and Spirits of the Stars, O all ye Angels and Elementary Spirits, O all ye Spirits present before the Face of God,

I the Minister and faithful Servant of the Most High conjure ye, let God Himself, the Existence of Existences, conjure ye to come and be present at this Operation, I, the Servant of God, most humbly entreat ye. Amen.

Having then caused the workmen to fill in the hole, thou shalt license the Spirits to depart, thanking them for the favour they have shown unto thee, and saying:--

The License to Depart: O ye good and happy Spirits, we thank ye for the benefits which we have just received from your liberal bounty; depart ye in peace to govern the Element which God hath destined for your habitation. Amen.

From **Veritable Dragon Noir: Black Dragon** (translation by Steve Savedow, Hadean Press, 2025. This particular spell is also included in *Grimorium Verum* and *The Grimoire of Pope Honorius*):

The Hand of Glory

Giving you gold and silver at will

Tear out the hair with its root from a mare in heat closest to nature; while saying: 'Dragne, Dragne', tighten this hair. Also go buy a new earthenware pot with its lid, without haggling. Go home, fill this pot with fountain water to two fingers near the edge, and put the said hair in it. Cover the pot and put it in a place that you and others cannot see it, because there would be danger.

At the end of nine days and at the same time of day that you hid it, go recover the pot. You will find inside a small animal in the shape of a snake which will stand upright, and to which you will immediately say: 'I accept the Pact.' That is, you will take it without touching it with your hand, and put it in a new box bought expressly (for this purpose), without haggling. You will give it wheat bran, nothing else, but you must not fail to give it every day. When you want to have silver or gold, you will put in the box as much as you want to have, and you will lie down on your bed

THE HIDDEN AND TRUE PNEUMATOLOGY

putting your box near you. Sleep if you want three or four hours and at the end of this time, you will find double the money as what you would have put there, but you have to be careful to put the same (amount) back.

Note that the little snake-shaped figure only comes by force of the charm, and you cannot put more than a hundred pounds[270] in it at a time. If, however, your planet gives you an influence over supernatural things, the serpent will have a face approaching the human figure, and you will be able to put up to a thousand pounds every day, you will get double it. If we want to get rid of it, we can give it to whoever we want as long as the person to whom you offer accepts it. Otherwise, the signs and characters of Figure 19 on virgin parchment will be put in the box and given to the little animal instead of the ordinary wheat bran. Give bran from flour on which the priest will have said his first Mass, and it will die. Take care not to forget any circumstance, for there is no mockery in this matter.

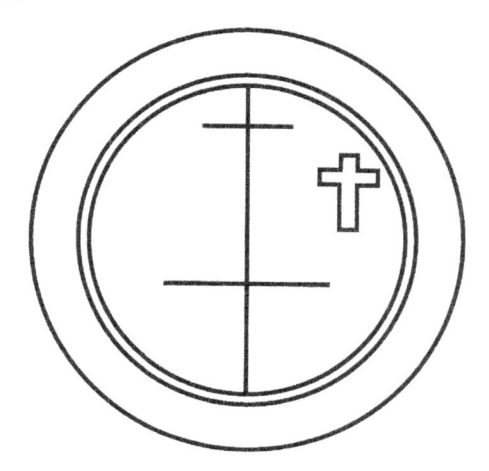

---

270 Translator's note: "mettre plus de cent livres."

From ***Albertus Magnus; Being the Approved, Verified, Sympathetic and Natural Egyptian Secrets: White and Black Art For Man and Beast***, etc. (Chicago: De Laurence Co., 1919):

Account of an Experienced Fortune Hunter, How Treasures Beneath the Earth Rise and Fall

If one is contemplating to dig up a treasure, he should above all other things know, whenever the treasure stands highest, to rise with the sun and return again with the sinking of the same. If the treasure happens to be hidden in an open field, the affair will soon be righted by digging around, crosswise, or undermining, so that the treasure can be reached from below, but one must not he tardy in constructing the posts or galleries in order to prop the treasure in time, because the digger might otherwise be buried underneath the falling heap. But, if it can he so conducted that the sun can shine crosswise under the treasure, it may be raised, since the goblins of the earth have no longer the power to remove the same.

From ***The Supreme Black, Red and Infernal Magic of the Egyptians and Chaldeans*** (translation by Steve Savedow, Hadean Press, 2022):

Magic Candle

If you know or have dreamed that there is a hidden treasure in a certain place, to find it will be necessary that you make a thick human tallow candle, placing it in a hole that you will make in the center of a piece of hazelnut wood, cut in the shape of a horseshoe.

Lit in the underground where you are looking for the treasure, the flame will indicate to you by its oscillation and crackling that you are approaching it, extinguishing when you are on top of the object of your yearnings.

THE HIDDEN AND TRUE PNEUMATOLOGY

From ***Treasure of the Old Man of the Pyramids*** (translation by Steve Savedow, Hadean Press, 2024):

PLANCHE 5.

Onaim, Pérantéſ, Raſonaſtoſ.

This plate represents the third of the talismans in the collection of the old man of the pyramids.[271]

The ring which must be used at the same time, will have a green stone of round shape with facets.[272]

You will engrave inside, the words traced at the bottom of plate 5.

---

[271] See *True Black Magic*, translated by Joseph Peterson, page 112, the fifth pentacle of Jupiter, for reliable visions in dreams.

[272] Possibly an emerald.

The talisman is used to discover treasures, and to ensure possession of them for your family.

For this it is necessary to place the ring on the second finger of the right hand, and to hold the talisman with the thumb and the little finger of the left hand while saying: 'Onaim, Perantes, Rasonastos'. At that time seven genies will appear, each with a large sack made of skin[273] which they will empty at your feet. These sacks will be full of the gold which they will have procured with the aid of a black owl, one of which will certainly accompany (them).[274]

To dismiss these genies, simply wave at them with your right hand.

From ***Petit Albert*** (translation by Steve Savedow, Hadean Press, 2025):

Those who have traveled to the northern countries and, above all, to Lapland,[275] cannot ignore the services that the gnomes render to the inhabitants of these regions, either to protect them from perils by warning them when they work, of the next landslides, or by (making them) know the places where mines are more abundant in precious metals.

The Lapps are so used to the frequent appearances of gnomes that, far from being frightened by them, they are sad when they do not appear when working in the mines, because it is a mark that

---

273 "sac de peau".

274 "d'une chouette noire, dont l'un sera bien certainement accompagne". See Plate 23 regarding the Black Owl. Also, in *The Black Pullet*, page 38, it states "Place the ring on the second finger of your right hand, enclose the talisman with the thumb and little finger of your left hand, and say 'Onaim, Perantes, Rasonastos. I repeated these three words and seven spirits of a bronze color appeared, each carrying a large hide bag which they emptied at my feet. etc."

275 Lapland or Sápmi, an ethno-cultural region stretching over northern Fennoscandia (parts of Norway, Sweden, Finland, and Russia).

these mines are sterile in metals when the gnomes do not make their residence there. It is a popular claim that the Creator has committed them to the custody of underground treasures, and that they have the faculty to dispense them as they see fit.

Those who are occupied in the discovery of gold and silver mines observe some ceremonies to gain the benevolence of the gnomes, so they are not opposed to them in their undertakings. Experience has taught that they are very fond of perfumes, and this is why the wise cabalists ordered them to be specific to each day of the week in relation to the seven planets. As I know from experience, many people have succeeded in discovering treasures by means of these perfumes. I am willing in favor of my readers to give them the real way of making them, so they can be agreeable to gnomes, guardians of these treasures; because it is necessary to know of all the creatures which inhabit the four elements, there are not some which are more resourceful[276] to harm or to do good to the men, according to the subjects (which one) gives them.

Perfume for Sunday under the auspices of the Sun.

All the perfumes should be made in a small new earthen stove, on charcoal of hazel[277] or laurel[278] to burn the perfume, but it must be lit by a fire which is made expressly with the pebble of a small gun.[279] It is good to observe that the pebble, the wick, the match and the candle are new, that they were not used for any profane use, for gnomes are extremely difficult and they are easily irritated. Saffron, as much aloe wood, as much balm wood, as much bay seed, as much cloves, as much myrtle, as much good

---

276 "ingenieuses".

277 Hazel (*Corylus*) is a genus of deciduous trees and large shrubs native to the temperate Northern Hemisphere.

278 Laurel is part of the English common name of many trees and other plants, particularly those of the laurel family (*Lauraceae*).

279 "petit fusil".

incense, a grain of musk, a grain of ambergris. Spray and mix together all these ingredients and form small grains[280] with a little tragacanth soaked in rose water. When they are very dry, use them occasionally by throwing three (grains) at a time on the hot coals.

Perfume for Monday under the auspices of the Moon.

This perfume must be formed with the following: take the head of a green frog, the apple of the eye of a white bull, white poppy seed, the most exquisite incense, such as storax, benzoin or frankincense, with a little camphor. Spray all these and mix them well together. Form a paste with the blood of a young goose or a turtledove. From this paste, form small grains to use three times, when they are very dry.

Perfume for Tuesday under the auspices of Mars.

This scent should be composed of spurge, bdellium, ammonia salt, herbore roots,[281] magnet stone powder, and a little flower of sulfur. Spray everything together, and make a paste with black cat's blood and crow's brain. From this paste, form grains to use three times on occasions.

Perfume of Wednesday, under the auspices of Mercury.

This perfume must be composed of ash seeds, aloe wood, good storax, benzoin, azure powder, and bits of peacock feathers. Spray and incorporate these ingredients with swallow blood and some deer brain. Make a paste of it and from this paste, form small grains to use three times on occasions, when they are dry.

Perfume for Friday under the auspices of Venus.

This scent must be musk, ambergris, aloe wood, dried roses, red coral. Spray all these and mix them together with dove or

---

280 "des petits grains".
281 Probably hellebore.

turtledove blood and the brains of two or three passerines.[282] Make a paste of it and from this paste, form small grains to use three times on occasions, when they are very dry.

Perfume of Saturday, under the auspices of Saturn.
The scent should consist of black poppy seeds, henbane, mandrake root, magnetite powder and good myrtle. Spray all these ingredients well, and mix them together with bat blood and black cat brains. Make a paste of it, and from this paste, form small grains to use three of them on occasions, when they are very dry.

We said—before giving the manner of making these perfumes—that the gnomes are, of all the creatures which inhabit the four elements, the most resourceful to do good or to harm men, according to the subjects they are given. This is why those who work in minerals or in search of treasures, being warned of this, do whatever they can to make them agreeable and take precautions as much as they can, against the effects of their indignation. Experience has shown several times that verbena and bay leaf are of good use in preventing gnomes from interfering with the work of those busy searching for treasures underground. Here is how Jamblic[283] and the *Arbatel*[284] talks about it in their cabalistic secrets.

When by natural or supernatural clues, that is to say by the revelation made in a dream, you are sure of the place where there will be a treasure; then make on this place, the proper perfume for

---

282 A passerine is any bird of the order *Passeriformes*, from the Latin *passer* or 'sparrow' and *formis* 'shaped', which includes more than half of all bird species. Sometimes known as perching birds or songbirds, passerines are distinguished from other orders of birds by the arrangement of their toes (three pointing forward and one back), which facilitates perching.

283 Iamblichus (245–325 CE).

284 The *Arbatel De Magia Veterum* was a Latin grimoire of Renaissance ceremonial magic published in 1575 in Switzerland, and later translated by Robert Turner in 1655.

the day when you want to start digging in the earth. Then you will plant, on the right hand (side) a branch of green laurel, and on the left hand (side), a branch of verbena. Then make the opening of the earth between these two branches. When you have made a hollow of your entire height, make a crown of these two branches, which you will wrap around your hat or bonnet. Above this crown, attach the talisman which I will give you the model here. If there are several (people), everyone must have the same crown.

It can be done on a fine tin plate, well purified on the day and at the hour of Jupiter. The theme of the sky being in a favorable situation. We will form it, on the one side the figure of fortune as it is represented here, and on the other side, these words in large characters:

OMOUZIN ALBOMATATOS

If working for several days before arriving to the place (where) the treasure is, we will renew each day the perfume which is specific to the day, as explained above. These precautions will ensure that the gnomes, guardians of the treasure, will not be harmful, and will even help you in your undertakings. It is a test of which I was an eye witness, with a favorable success in the old castle of Orviete.

Also, see the following texts for various spells and formulae regarding the location and acquisition of "hidden treasures" (see bibliography for information on these texts):

Book Of Oberon: A Sourcebook Of Elizabethan Magic
Book Of the Sacred Magic Of Abramelin The Mage
Book Of Saint Cyprian: The Sorcerer's Treasure
Picatrix: A Medieval Treatise On Astral Magic
Three Books Of Occult Philosophy
Fourth Book Of Occult Philosophy
Sworn Book Of Honorius The Magician
Grimoire Of Arthur Gauntlet

Appendix C

BIBLICAL REFERENCES

This is Psalm 91 as taken from the King James Bible:

PSALM 91

1. He that dwelleth in the secret place of the most High shall abide under the shadow of the Almighty.
2. I will say of the Lord, He is my refuge and my fortress: my God; in him will I trust.
3. Surely he shall deliver thee from the snare of the fowler, and from the noisome pestilence.
4. He shall cover thee with his feathers, and under his wings shalt thou trust: his truth shall be thy shield and buckler.
5. Thou shalt not be afraid for the terror by night; nor for the arrow that flieth by day;
6. Nor for the pestilence that walketh in darkness; nor for the destruction that wasteth at noonday.
7. A thousand shall fall at thy side, and ten thousand at thy right hand; but it shall not come nigh thee.
8. Only with thine eyes shalt thou behold and see the reward of the wicked.
9. Because thou hast made the Lord, which is my refuge, even the most High, thy habitation;
10. There shall no evil befall thee, neither shall any plague come nigh thy dwelling.
11. For he shall give his angels charge over thee, to keep thee in all thy ways.
12. They shall bear thee up in their hands, lest thou dash thy foot against a stone.
13. Thou shalt tread upon the lion and adder: the young lion and the dragon shalt thou trample under feet.

14. Because he hath set his love upon me, therefore will I deliver him: I will set him on high, because he hath known my name.

15. He shall call upon me, and I will answer him: I will be with him in trouble; I will deliver him, and honour him.

16. With long life will I satisfy him, and shew him my salvation.

The Twelve Articles of the Christian Faith

I believe in God the Father almighty,
Creator of heaven and earth.
And in Jesus Christ, His only Son,
our Lord, Who was conceived by the Holy Spirit,
born of the Virgin Mary,
suffered under Pontius Pilate,
was crucified, died, and was buried.
He descended into hell; the third day
He rose again from the dead;
He ascended into heaven, and sits at
the right hand of God the Father
almighty, from thence He shall come
to judge the living and the dead.
I believe in the Holy Spirit,
the holy Catholic Church,
the communion of saints,
the forgiveness of sins,
the resurrection of the body
and life everlasting.
Amen.

Bibliography

Albertus Magnus; Being the Approved, Verified, Sympathetic & Natural Egyptian Secrets: White & Black Art for Man & Beast etc., Chicago: De Laurence Co., 1919.

Arbatel; Concerning the Magic of the Ancients: Original Sourcbook of Angel Magic, Ibis Press, 2009, newly translated, edited & annotated by Joseph H. Peterson.

Arbatel of Magick, Heptangle Books, 1979, translation by Robert Turner.

Aurea Catena Homeri, Sapere Aude Metaphysical Republishers, 1983, translation by Sigismund Bacstrom.

The Black Books of Elverum, Galde Press, 1999, edited & translated by Mary S. Rustad.

The Black Raven or the Threefold Coercion of Hell, independently published, 2019, editor Brittany Nightshade.

The Book of Abramelin: A New Translation; Being a Complete & Accurate Presentation From Extant Manuscripts, Including the First Publication of Its Fourth Part, Ibis Press, 2006, revised & expanded 2nd edition 2015, compiled & edited by Georg Dehn, translated by Steven Guth.

The Book of Enoch, Oxford: Clarendon Press, 1912, editor & translator R.H. Charles.

The Book of the Sacred Magic of Abra-Melin the Mage, London: John Watkins, 1889, translation by S.L. MacGregor Mathers.

The Book of Saint Cyprian: The Sorcerer's Treasure, Hadean Press, 2014, translated with commentary by Jose Leitao.

The Book of Tobit from the Apocrypha, Middlesex: Raven Press, 1931, illustrator Horace Walter Bray.

The Book of Treasure Secrets: A Grimoire of Magical Conjurations to Reveal Treasure & Catch Thieves by Invoking Spirits, Fallen Angels, Demons & Fairies, Avalonia Publishing, 2009, edited by David Rankine.

Das Kloster; Weltlich und Geistlich; Meist aus der Altern Deutschen Volks-, Wunder-, Curiositaten-, und Vorzugsweise Komischen Literatur, Stuttgart: Selbstverlag, 1845–1849, edited by Johann Scheible.

Elucidation of Necromancy: Lucidarium Arti Nigromantice - Attributed to Peter De Abano, Ibis Press 2021, translation & commentary by Joseph H. Peterson.

Goetia: Lesser Key of Solomon the King, Society for the Propagation of Religious Truth, 1904, transcribed by S.L. MacGregor Mathers, but attributed to Aleister Crowley.

Golden Chain of Homer, CreateSpace, 2015.

The Grand Grimoire: A Practical Manual of Diabolic Evocation & Black Magic; The Grand Clavicule of Solomon; The Black Magick or the Infernal Arts of the Great Agrippa to Discover All Hidden Treasures & to Render All of the Spirits Obedient to Oneself, Trident Books, 2004, translated by Gretchen Rudy.

The Grand Grimoire; Being a Source Book of Magical Incidents & Diabolical Pacts, Holmes Publishing, 2010, 4th edition, revised, compiled & edited by Darcy Kuntz.

The Great Grimoire of Pope Honorius, Trident Books, 1999, translated from the German by Kineta Ch'ien, additional translation by Matthew Sullivan.

The Grimoire of Arthur Gauntlet: A 17th Century London Cunning-Man's Book of Charms, Conjurations & Prayers, Avalonia, 2011, editor David Rankine.

The Grimoire of Pope Honorius, English Edition, Dark Arts Publishing, 2019, edited & translated by Edmund Kelly.

The Grimoire of St. Cyprian, English Edition, Dark Arts Publishing, 2019, edited & translated by Edmund Kelly.

Grimorium Verum: A Handbook of Black Magic, Createspace Publishing, 2007, edited & translated by Joseph Peterson.

Grimoirium Verum: Containing the Most Approved Keys of Solomon Wherein the Most Hidden Secrets Both Natural & Supernatural Are Immediately Exhibited, Trident Books, 1994.

Heptameron or Magical Elements of Peter De Abano, Ouroboros Press, 2003, translated into English by Robert Turner.

Holy Bible: King James Version, Hendrickson Publishing, 2004.

Iamblichus on the Mysteries of the Egyptians, Chaldeans and Assyrians, Wizards Bookshelf, 1997, translation by Thomas Taylor.

The Key of Solomon the King, Weiser Inc., 2000, translation by S.L. MacGregor Mathers.

The Lesser Key of Solomon: Lemegeton Clavicula Salomonis; Detailing the Ceremonial Art of Commanding Spirits Both Good & Evil, Weiser Books, 2001, edited by Joseph H. Peterson.

Petit Albert & Albert D'grand, Hadean Press (forthcoming), translation by Steve Savedow.

Picatrix: A Medieval Treatise on Astral Magic, Penn State University Press, 2019, translation & introduction by Dan Attrel & David Porreca.

Picatrix: Ghayat Al-Hakim: The Goal of the Wise, Volume One, Ouroboros Press, 2002, translated from the Arabic by Hashem Atallah, edited by William Keisel.

Picatrix: Ghayat Al-Hakim: The Goal of the Wise, Volume Two, Ouroboros Press, 2008, translated from the Arabic by Hashem Atallah & Geylan Holmquest, edited by William Keisel.

Plotinus: The Enneads, Cambridge University Press, 2017, edited and translated by Lloyd Gerson et al.

The Secret Grimoire of Turiel, Aquarian Press, 1960, attributed to Marius Malchus.

The Sixth & Seventh Books of Moses, Ibis Press, 2008, edited by Joseph Peterson.

The Supreme Black, Red and Infernal Magic of the Egyptians and Chaldeans, Hadean Press, 2022, translation by Steve Savedow.

The Sword Of Moses: An Ancient Book of Magic, From a Unique Manuscript, Weiser Inc., 1970, introduction & translation by Moses Gaster.

The Sworn Book of Honourius the Magician; As Composed by Honourius Through Counsel With the Angel Hocroell, Heptangle Books, 1977.

The Sworn Book of Honorius; Liber Iuratus Honorii, Ibis Press, 2016, translation & commentary by Joseph Peterson.

Thabit Ibn Qurra On Talismans *& Ps.- Ptolemyon* On Images *1 – 9. Together With the* Liber Prestigiorum Thebidis *of Adelard of Bath*, Sismel—edizioni del galluzzo, 2021, edited by Gideon Bohak & Charles Burnett.

Veritable Dragon Noir: Black Dragon, Hadean Press (forthcoming), translation by Steve Savedow.

The Veritable Key of Solomon, Golden Hoard Publications, 2017, editors Stephen Skinner & David Rankine.

Zauber-Bibliothek: Oder, Von Zauberei, Theurgie und Mantik, Zauberern, Hexen, und Hexenprocessen, Damonen, Gespenstern, und Geistererscheinungen, Mainz: Verlag Florian Kupferberg, 1821–1826, six volumes, edited by Georg Conrad Horst.

Acher, Frater, *Speculum Terrae: A Magical Earth-Mirror From The 17th Century*, Hadean Press, 2018.

Agrippa, Henry Cornelius (attributed), *Fourth Book of Occult Philosophy*, Ibis Press, 2015, translated into English by Robert Turner, edited with commentary & introduction by Stephen Skinner.

Agrippa, Henry Cornelius (attributed), *Of Occult Philosophy, Book Four, Magical Ceremonies*, Heptangle Books, 1985.

Agrippa, Heinrich Cornelius, *Three Books of Occult Philosophy*, Inner Traditions, 2021, translated from the original Latin edition of 1533 by Eric Purdue.

Agrippa, Henry Cornelius, *Three Books Of Occult Philosophy*, Llewelyn, 1993/2019, translated by James Freake, edited & annotated by Donald Tyson.

Alighieri, Dante, *Divine Comedy*, Verona: Edizioni Valdonega, 2007, translation by Robert Hollander.

Barrett, Francis, *The Magus, or Celestial Intelligencer*, London: Lackington, Allen, and Co, 1801; Thorsons Publishers Ltd, 1980.

Bulfinch, Thomas, *Bulfinch's Mythology*, Spring Books, 1967.

Ceccetelli, Michael, *Crossed Keys*, Scarlet Imprint, 2010, English translation of *Le Veritable Dragon Noir* and *Enchiridion of Pope Leo III*.

Davidson, Gustav, *A Dictionary of Angels, Including the Fallen Angels*, Free Press, 1967.

De Plancy, Collin Jacques, *Dictionnaire Infernal*, Paris: Henri Plon, 1863, 6th edition.

De Plancy, J. Collin, *Infernal Dictionary: A Universal Directory*, Abracax House, 2015–2016, translation & annotations by Natalia Zasadzineka, Jean-Christophe Dufau, Michal Coles.

De Teramo, Jacobus, *Das Buch Belial*, Augsberg, 1473.

Gilbert, R.A., *Sorcerer & His Apprentice*, Aquarian Press, 1983.

Harms, Daniel; Clark, James R.; Peterson, Joseph H., *The Book of Oberon: A Sourcebook of Elizabethan Magic*, Llewelyn Publishing, 2019.

Hay, George, *Necronomicon: Book of Dead Names*, Neville Spearman, 1978.

Heywood, Thomas, *Hierarchie of the Blessed Angells: Their Names, Orders & Offices, the Fall of Lucifer With His Angels*, etc., London, 1635.

Lovecraft, Howard Phillips, *Beyond the Wall of Sleep*, Arkham House, 1943.

Milton, John, *Paradise Lost: A Poem Written in Ten Books*, London, 1667.

Savedow, Steve, *Goetic Evocation*, Eschaton Productions, 1996; Hadean Press, 2022.
Simon, *Necronomicon*, Schlangekraft Inc./Barnes Graphics, 1977.
Trachtenberg, Joshua, *Jewish Magic and Superstition*, Behrmans, 1939.
Von Eckartshausen, Karl, *Magic: The Principles of Higher Knowledge*, Merkur Publishing, 1989, translated into English and edited by Gerhard Hanswille & Deborah Brumlich.

Milton Keynes UK
Ingram Content Group UK Ltd.
UKHW010713311023
431661UK00001B/52